Christmas Eve at Central Lutheran Church, Minneapolis.
Photo by Don Mueller.

WHAT GOD HATH WROUGHT

The Motto of
CENTRAL LUTHERAN CHURCH

"The Faith of the Fathers in the Language of the Children." Twentieth Century American methods, but explicit obedience to Our Lord.

The changing order, but the never-changing Word of God.

—From Central's Yearbook for 1920

WHAT GOD HATH WROUGHT

The Story of
CENTRAL LUTHERAN CHURCH
in Minneapolis

*"God Works in a Mysterious Way His Wonders
to Perform"*

Written By
LAWRENCE M. BRINGS, M.A.

Publishers
T. S. DENISON & COMPANY, INC.
Minneapolis

DEDICATION

We, the family of God in Central Lutheran Church, dedicate this book —

To the glory of God, the Father, Son and Holy Spirit, for His mercy and grace these sixty years —

To our faithful pastors and dedicated workers who have fought the good fight of faith —

To the future of our church that those who come after us may carry onward that which has already been established, to ever greater success, that God may be more fully glorified.

ACKNOWLEDGMENTS

The author wishes to acknowledge his appreciation to the many individuals who assisted in the research involved in the preparation of this book, particularly to the members of the Official History Committee for the Fiftieth Anniversary of Central Church: Esther Gehrke, chairman; Cordelia Baisner, Lillian Anderson, Mrs. Merlin Hovden, and Mrs. Serine Prestholdt;

To Dr. L. E. Leipold for his valuable assistance in organizing the data compiled for this book.

To Mr. Leif R. Larson who directed the classification of all the official documents of the church;

To Emil Johansen, Christian Wangaard and Oliver Prestholdt who furnished recollections of the early beginnings of the church;

To the pastors of the church, past and present, who shared their observations with us;

And to the numerous members who encouraged us in the task of bringing this story of religious adventure to realization.

— THE AUTHOR

CONTENTS

CHAPTER 1

In the Beginning — A Great Adventure

"The beginning remains always the most notable event." — Carlyle

This is the story of a church. In itself, this is not important. It is more significant that it is the romantic story of a great church. They who founded it were men of vision, those who followed were rich in faith. The cornerstone upon which the structure rested was service to others.

Built upon this solid rock, the church prospered and grew, enriching the lives of the many people with whom it came in contact.

The year was 1917. America was embroiled in the unhappy affairs of rival European nations and was at war. It was a stirring time, for the American people believed in the cause for which they were fighting. To them, it was a war to end wars. Peace and victory would bring a new era to a distressed world, they believed, and they worked hard to bring this ideal about.

In the city of Minneapolis there was a small group of men who were disturbed about another matter. They felt in their hearts the need for a church that would fulfill the unique purpose which they hoped could be achieved. It must be like no other church that was then to be found in the city. It must be Lutheran, they declared, and it must serve the downtown area. Then they added a significant third requirement: it must be a church with a mission of service. No lesser criteria would suffice. Give them such a church and they would rejoice. They were determined to accept nothing less.

So it was that in an era of strife, a church of peace was founded. In the beginning it was only a dream and a hope, an idea conceived in the minds of men. This is true of all great achievements. The idea then becomes a plan and the plan becomes a fact. At first there was no church; then because somebody cared, there was one that filled a need.

Minneapolis was then, as it is now, Minnesota's largest city. Four hundred thousand people resided within its borders. It was a busy city of flour mills and railroad terminals, of banks and fine stores. Little more than a half century had elapsed since the first settlers had carved a village out of the virgin woods. It was at a strategic spot where the Falls of St. Anthony tumbled the Mississippi waters over its rough edge. The falls provided limitless power to turn the wheels of the mills that ground the wheat raised on sprawling prairie farms into flour which in turn was shipped to the far corners of the earth. Forests were ruthlessly cut down to keep the sawmills running, and lumbering was as important an industry as was milling.

In only a half century Minneapolis had grown from a river-landing town to a proud metropolis, serving an area that extended as far west as Montana and north into the vast reaches of Canada.

Minneapolis in the year 1917 was a city grown up. In some ways it was already feeling the effects of age. The original settlement which centered about the Falls of St. Anthony was now becoming old, its buildings of a style of another era. The business district was pushing steadily southward, away from the river. What had been only a short time ago the outer fringes of the town became the center of a new business district. Apartment houses replaced one-family dwellings and a new type of living accommodation developed. Streetcars, serving the residential districts, came downtown to turn around, and a new term was applied to that bustling business district. It was called "the loop."

By 1917 there were thousands of residents living in the apartment houses of the Minneapolis downtown area. Men and women, coming to this largest city of the Northwest, arrived by train, and being strangers in the city, looked for dwelling places near the depot at which they disembarked. The automobile industry was in its first-decade infancy and the roads leading to the city were unsurfaced and unmarked. The airplane as yet was not a factor in the transportation field. The railroad was still the most important single means of getting from one point to another insofar as greater distances were concerned. When people from "outstate" came to Minneapolis, they invariably came by train.

Living in the loop area were thousands of families and still greater numbers of single men and women. Many of them had no church home. It was these people with whom the small group of sincere men, who wanted to found a new and unique church, were concerned. They knew well the needs of the residents of the area. However, people were busy and the times were hectic. The men talked and planned for a time, but no further action was taken.

Then the war ended. A new inflex of people arrived in the city. A great restlessness prevailed. Young men and women who had known only rural life before came home from military service and were no longer satisfied with farm and small-town life.

"How're you going to keep them down on the farm, after they've seen Paree?" asked the songwriter, and the young people, released from military restrictions, replied, "You can't!" They headed for the cities in droves, and Minneapolis received its full share.

The transition from rural to urban life was for them a confusing one. The spaciousness of farms that they knew so well was replaced by the restrictions of the city. Country trails and city streets had little in common. Friends and relatives of former days were far away; suddenly missing were the associations of a lifetime. Sorely missed also was the church which had for so long filled a need in their lives. In the apartment jungles of the loop, churches often became a thing apart and the habits of a lifetime were sometimes quickly forgotten.

The men who had long thought of the necessity of a special kind of church to meet the needs of the loop residents knew that the time had now come when action must replace words. They would begin a church that was new in form and purpose. It would not be an offshoot of any other church body nor would it be an amalgamation.

It must have its beginning then and there, becoming a church to meet the needs of a special area, regardless of belief or membership. It would be Lutheran, but it would serve all people. This was their purpose and their intent.

With Mr. S. H. Holstad acting as temporary chairman, several meetings were held by the men dedicated to this philosophy. They proceeded with their plans without any assistance from a home missions board, a synodical directive, or a "mother" congregation to guide them. They organized as a permanent committee on Jan. 3, 1919, to start an all-English Lutheran church in downtown Minneapolis.

The founders were John H. Field, O. L. Loberg, Dr. F. Moody, S. A. Nelson, Oliver Prestholdt, Dr. Ivar Sivertsen, Dr. C. O. Solberg, J. S. Strate, E. H. Sund, Dr. A. C. Tingdale, R. T. Tingdale and Christian Wangaard. These men and their families constituted the entire congregation until May when additional charter members were added. The founders became the church trustees and activities of the congregation began in earnest.

Recently vacated was the building which formerly housed the Central Baptist Church. Located on Grant Street and Fourth Avenue, at the south edge of the Loop, its congregation had decided to combine with another church body and the building was available for other purposes. Could one group succeed where another had given up the struggle? Time alone would tell, but the faith of the small group was great. They had an idea which they proposed to test in the front line of action.

The church would be Lutheran, but the services must be in English. First generation settlers from the predominantly Lutheran countries of north Europe were no longer as numerous as they once had been in Minnesota. When they first came to America, the customs and mores of the mother country continued to guide their ways. In most of the churches the native language continued to be spoken for many years. With the coming of the war, a wave of nationalism, of patriotic feeling for their adopted country, took place. Where Norwegian and Swedish and German services had long been held, the English language replaced the mother tongue. For this reason the new church must use only the English language. Only then would it have appeal for all people, regardless of ancestry.

Also high on the list of the criteria that was to guide them was the requirement that it be a church that served all people, whether they be members or nonmembers, regardless of race or economic status. The day worker was to be as important a part of the church structure as his well-to-do employer; the single man or woman, as welcome as the married couple; the young as much a part of the group as the old. These were the guidelines established; these were the requirements which prevailed. This was a philosophy to be continued during the next sixty years.

It had been hoped that as many as thirty or forty families would form the nucleus of the new organization, but when the roll was taken and the time came to stand up and be counted, only twelve families were present to form the compact. Only twelve, a discouragingly small number to begin such an ambitious project, to commit their word and bond to a binding deed.

When this time came, not one of the families became faint-hearted and said, "It is better that we wait for a more fitting day to come." Twelve men with faith were stronger in purpose than ten times that number with faint hearts.

So it was that in the year 1919, Central Lutheran Church of Minneapolis was born. Its first building had been the Central Baptist; now it was Central Lutheran.

"It is better that we keep the name 'Central,'" they agreed, "for it shall be our purpose, to serve the central part of our city."

So began the story of service that has completed a full sixty years. It is filled with the spirit of sacrifice. It commands an enviable place among the histories of other churches, not only in the city of Minneapolis, but throughout the nation. Seldom has a small handful of men and women been privileged to see the fruits of their endeavors so gloriously ripened.

At the beginning of their service, there were only the few; today there are thousands, while tens of thousands have been served through the passing years. They began with no church structure and no minister. Today they have a beautiful edifice and a full complement of staff workers. The most significant achievement is recorded not in material growth, but in the spiritual investments made in the hearts of the many who have been touched by the spirit of Christ, in whose name this work has been done.

A decade and a half after Central Lutheran Church was founded, the question was asked, "How has all of this been brought about?" The answer was given: "Through faith in God; the vision of a pressing need; the grasping of an opportunity; the sacrifice, loyalty, and liberality of all associated with Central from its beginning to the present time; and the able and masterful leadership of a man of

God, whose heart and soul and talents have been dedicated to Central and a life of service."

The person referred to here was Pastor J. A. O. Stub, first minister of Central Lutheran Church, and of whom much more will be written in this history.

Now after sixty years, Central stands as a proud monument to the victory of courage over temporal handicaps. It is a twentieth-century example of Christian service in the truest sense of the term, broad in scope, firmly established in the Faith, simple in its fellowship, in competition with no other church, but working in harmony with all others; all co-laborers in the Master's business whatever their creed or Christian denomination.

Throughout its first sixty years, this church has stressed but one great fundamental belief: *Salvation* through faith in the shed blood of *Jesus Christ, Son of God.* Yet this church has not forgotten nor does it pass by, the temporal ills that man is heir to or the friendly social intercourse which is so much an inherent part of the lives of a free and happy people. It cares for those in need to the limit of its resources and joins in the spirit of thankfulness and joy of those whose needs have been met. Through all of its years it has both preached and practiced the gospel of Jesus Christ without equivocation. Its sympathies have remained from the beginning as broad as humanity itself.

Central has rejoiced in the leadership of great men and women, but is has never been a "one-man" church. It has been truly democratic, yielding to the principles of Americanism at all times. Its ideals have been those of our nation, yielding to no class but being ever all-inclusive. Although its membership, adherents and friends have been the descendants of nationals speaking many tongues, its services and meetings have been conducted only in the language of America.

Although Central Lutheran Church began humbly, as was fitting, its influence and service have expanded in ever-widening circles.

CHAPTER 2

The First Year

"Twelve Courageous Men With a Dream"

It is significant to observe that during the preliminary discussions of the twelve founders, it was their unanimous decision that the new church should be different — entirely the reverse of the common practice of the neighborhood church of that day. No longer was the pastor to carry the entire load of responsibility in all the affairs of the congregation; it was to be shared by the members. His role was to care for the spiritual needs of people in the community, members and nonmembers alike. The laymen were to provide the physical facilities and the finances to meet the challenge of service in the community. It has been a continuing policy during the subsequent years to define the duties and responsibilities of the pastoral staff and the laymen in these two categories.

Central Lutheran Church is not and never has been, dominated by any single individual, either layman or pastor.

It is, nevertheless, true that throughout its sixty years of service there have been those workers who have stood taller than their contemporaries. These men and women labored in the field, serving their church with devotion and leaving the good of their services behind when they departed. Their church and their community — and the lives of many persons — have been the better because they passed this way. While they stood out among their fellow workers, their great contributions were but a part of the whole achievement of their common endeavors. They worked with others to bring to fruition the goals of the church, and they were not alone in their endeavors.

Such a man among men was Central's first pastor, the Rev. Dr. J. A. O. Stub. From his installation on Palm Sunday in the year 1919 until his death a quarter of a century later, his life was dedicated to the welfare of his church. He guided, yet he did not direct; he recommended, but he did not order. He possessed the remarkable facility of inspiring the members of the congregation to actively participate in the areas of their interest and ability. He never demanded; he always suggested how an individual could better serve his God and church. Through the first critical years of Central Lutheran, his firm hand was always there, giving faith and reliance to the work at hand. When he departed, so well had his role been played that the work went on to new and greater heights. No story of this church would be complete without a recognition of the services performed by this stalwart man of God.

In his own humble words, Pastor Stub has told his own story as it is recorded in the archives of the church.

"I come from a long line of clergy ancestors," he said. "There were 43 of my father's ancestors who were clergymen, and 44 of my mother's."

"My father was a revered patriarch, the Rev. Dr. H. G. Stub, president of the Norwegian Lutheran Church of America. He was a pioneer of what was then the West and was born in a log cabin in the state of Wisconsin, and so was my mother. Most of the recollections that I have of my childhood are connected with the church. I grew up in my grandparents' home, as my mother died when I was only two years old. It was there, and later in my father's home, that I acquired the ideal that had guided my life: 'The Church is the most important thing in my life.' From thence onward, the work of the church has had first place in my life. Many are the sacrifices that were made to keep this ideal alive in my heart, but I have never departed from it.

"When the United States entered the war in 1917, I felt at once that the church must follow the men in the service. I took a leave of absence and became a chaplain. One task led to another. I was soon appointed general executive of the National Lutheran Commission for Solders' and Sailors' Welfare. As such I had the management of the organized war work of the Lutheran Church and was responsible for the expenditure of $1,500,000 contributed by our people. I worked with all commissioned pastors and over 300 volunteer camp pastors . . . However, when the war ended, I yearned for the active ministry once again. My name had become well known in Lutheran circles and several calls were extended to me. One came from a large congregation with a flattering salary inducement. I was strongly tempted to take it, for I had a wife and four children to support. Then one day, I received a call from this little group of men in Minneapolis. It thrilled my imagination and it appealed to my heart. What faith they had! Twelve men with a dream! I could not help but believe that it was God's will that there should be a church of our faith, thoroughly American in spirit, method and practice, in the heart of Minneapolis. My heart thrilled at the thought that it was in this city that my father began his work as a young minister when Minneapolis had a population of only 30,000. Now it was a city of 400,000. So, in God's name and trusting in Him, my family and I burned our bridges and took the step."

Such was the character of the man who was to guide the destiny of Central Church from its birth through the hazardous years that followed.

Before accepting the call, Dr. Stub met with the organizers of the church and together they reached an understanding.

"I told the group of courageous men that if it were their intention to establish this church as a 'typical' Lutheran church of the Midwest, primarily as a neighborhood church, I was not interested. However, if it were their ambition under God to make it a downtown church, teeming with activity, meeting the needs of society as it exists in our large cities today, and if they were willing to stand by the ship for a period of five years in order to give it a fair trial, I would cast my lot with them and give them the best that I had. They agreed, and so our work began."

The building that had been the Central Baptist Church was rented, having just become vacant. Its congregation had given up, to become incorporated in two of the newer neighborhood churches. The first year's rent was paid in advance by the little group of hopeful founders. Another $2,000 was spent in cleaning and painting the old building and installing the luxury of a small amount of new carpeting.

The auditorium of the church seated five hundred and fifty persons — certainly an adequate capacity for a congregation having but a dozen families. There was also an adjoining Sunday school building which seated another five hundred. This could be opened into the main sanctuary, providing a seating capacity of well over a thousand worshippers. All of the usual church equipment was present, including a pipe organ.

The joy of the little congregation was great when the message of acceptance was received from Dr. Stub. Some of them had felt that it was almost an affront to the well-known pastor to extend a call from a congregation that existed in hope only, except for the founding handful, and at an annual salary of $2,500. Now the great man was their spiritual leader. What challenge it was for both pastor and congregation!

On Palm Sunday, April 13, 1919, Pastor Stub was installed. Officiating was President Dr. C. O. Solberg of the English Association. Assisting was Dr. Stub's father, who from the pulpit that day exhorted his son to steadfastly preach the gospel of Jesus Christ.

Four days later, on Thursday evening of Holy Week, the new church's first communion was celebrated. Augmenting well for the future, eighty-one partook of the Lord's Supper on that Maundy Thursday.

Easter Sunday dawned bright and fair. It was almost as if an omen were present. As the hour of holy service approached, the very streets were filled with men, women and children, converging upon Central Lutheran Church, now officially one week old. A miracle took place that Easter morning. The church edifice, deserted so shortly before, was filled to capacity. One week only had been needed to prove the wisdom of the church's founders. Their faith was justified.

It was decided that all members who joined Central before the end of the calendar year of 1919 should be recorded as charter members of the church. In

The Rev. J. A. O. Stub, D.D., 1924

First home of Central Lutheran Church, formerly the building of
the Central Baptist Church

The Chancel of "Old Central"

Women's Guild meeting, showing the auditorium of "Old Central"

The church parlors and Sunday School auditorium

The site of the Sanctuary

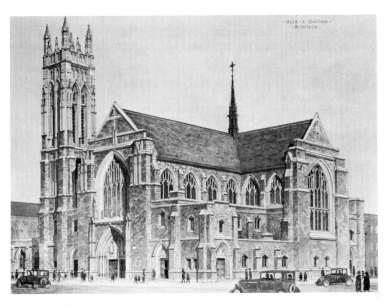

Architect's model for the new Sanctuary

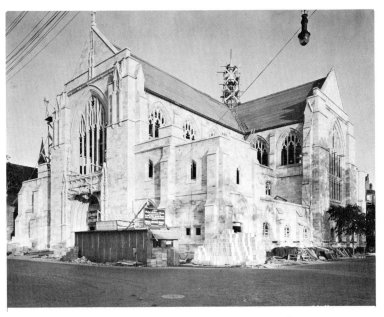

The Sanctuary in process of construction

Site of Sunday School building

Confirmation Class, June 5, 1938

Boy Scout Troop, 1942

December the number passed the five hundred mark. At year's end, the number stood at five hundred and forty-two, a remarkable record, indeed.

Pastor Stub was a masterful organizer, never at a loss to recruit the help of the members. In the autumn, a budget for the year 1920 was adopted, totaling $11,500. This budget was formally approved by the congregation. On the last Sunday of December, twenty-six teams of two men each, solicited the members for pledges for the coming year, securing fully three fourths of the funds needed. Before the year ended, this amount had been increased to over $9,000.

The question of whether the new church would or would not succeed had now been answered. On February 26, 1920, less than a year after the installation of Pastor Stub, the congregation, in meeting assembled, authorized the purchase of the church property for $33,000, payable in five annual installments. As a token of their good faith, eighty-one of those present pledged a total of $16,150 toward the buying of the land and building. When two weeks later, the twenty-six teams once more called on those who had not already pledged, another $9,000 was subscribed.

When the first anniversary of the founding of the church was reached, stock was taken of the accomplishments made. In retrospect, it seemed like a dream. On Palm Sunday, 1919, twelve families were members of Central. One year later, 220 families were on the membership roll, representing a total of 581 individuals, truly a remarkable record. In a voice choked with emotion, Pastor Stub said to his congregation that day, "This is the Lord's doing. It is marvelous in our eyes."

CHAPTER **3**

The Committee of Twelve Proposes a Sanctuary

"He builded better than he knew." —Emerson

Over sixty years in the long life of the Christian Church is but a short span of time. One wonders if the Man from Galilee, as he preached to the curious on the banks of the Jordan, knew then how far his doctrine would spread through the centuries. Instructing his followers to go even to the far corners of the earth to carry the new message of redemption, He himself never wandered far from his native city. He lived and died within the confines of a small and inhospitable land.

Little by little, the word spread from one country to another. It traveled a tragic road and the martyrs to the cause were many, but there was no power great enough to stop it. The end is not yet!

Central Lutheran Church has completed over sixty years of service, dedicated to the cause of spreading the Word of the Master Teacher. His message was clear and explicit: Tell the story of the Fatherhood of God and the Brotherhood of Man. Central was founded on this command.

Today there are not twelve men, as there were in 1919. Only one survived fifty years later. He was Christian Wangaard, who lived his declining years in the Ebenezer Home in his native city, only a short distance from the church that he helped to found. His memories of the years were long and pleasant.

A question that has come to the minds of many persons was asked him by the author:

"How did you twelve men first come together? Someone must have had an idea . . ."

His answer came from the recollections that are his from fifty years ago. The years have accentuated them, but they have not dimmed them.

"A group of us — we were friends, business associates, professional acquaintances — met first at the Odin Club one evening. Mr. J. H. Field first suggested that we meet to talk the matter over. Dr. Moody was there too, as was Mr. Prestholdt. I came because I felt the need, as they did. This was in 1917. Nothing tangible was accomplished that night, but the germ of an idea was planted and it would not be downed. It grew, the word passing from one person to another. Some were not interested. Those who were had a contagious enthusiasm that inspired others. We were but a few, we well knew, but our cause was a great one."

"Why did you think that you could do better than the congregation that gave up and combined forces with another church?" he was asked.

"We did feel that our goals were similar," he replied. "We wanted a downtown Lutheran church. There was none before Central was founded. We were denominational, but our appeal would be to every

Christian who did not have a church home. Try as we might to find flaws in our logic, it was difficult to do so. We inevitably came back to 'the same door by which we entered'; Minneapolis needs an English-speaking downtown Lutheran church that will serve everyone who has an interest in it. The congregation that gave up and left its building vacant was intensely denominational, intent upon serving its members. We sought to serve everyone in the community, regardless of race or creed. We, whose purpose was broad, succeeded where others with a narrow purpose failed."

"How did you secure the services of Dr. Stub?" he was asked. "Your first pastor, who was to fill such a vital role in determining the success of your church venture, was a man of wide reputation. He could well have accepted a call to a large, firmly established congregation. Instead, he came to Central, a small, struggling group which had in no way yet proved itself."

Again the reply was a definite one. "We had Dr. Stub in mind right from the start," he said. "There were several reasons for this. In the first place, we knew Dr. Stub's father, who occupied such a high place in the Lutheran church. We talked to him about our plans and he was thrilled. When we spoke of asking his son to come here to work with us, he was delighted. We felt that the father would be happy to have his son locate nearby rather than in a far-distant place. I believe that he caught some of our fervor and took a look into the future, seeing the same vision that we did. Also, some of us knew Dr. Stub personally, several knowing him since college days. He felt that he was among old friends when he came here. He could have had his pick of congregations, but he chose Central. It was to his credit — and to our advantage."

Another question came to mind that only this lone survivor of the original twelve founders could answer.

"Did you ever have any real doubts about Central's success?" he was asked.

There was a moment's reflection, then the answer came.

"Really we didn't," he said. "Our enthusiasm was high and we did not consider failure as one of the possibilities of our venture. Or, if any of us did, we really never admitted it either to ourselves or to others. I don't believe that any of us realized how rapidly our church would advance and prosper, but none of us considered failure as a possible outcome. I was treasurer at the time and there were uneasy days that came and went, I readily admit. Somehow we managed to meet our obligations. Our phenomenal attendance assured us very soon of enough income to keep solvent."

"What kind of a speaker was Dr. Stub?" was the final question put to the lone survivor of the organizer's group. "Was he a man with personal appeal?"

The reply came quickly. "That he was. He had a sincerity about his delivery and a strength to his faith that could be easily understood. *And he could be heard.* He did not need any loudspeaker, either. A group of us, all members of Sons of Norway, went to Winnipeg once to attend a conference. We were to have an outdoor session, but it began to rain just before services started and on the spur of the moment we took shelter in a large building with a metal roof. The rain came down in torrents and the noise was something to hear. The minister who was trying to preach the sermon had to give up; he just could not make himself heard above the din of the rain on the tin roof. Then we thought of Dr. Stub. Let him get up there and speak, we suggested. Unprepared as he was, he got up there and spoke and needed no loudspeaker to make himself heard. He always had something worthwhile to say and he knew how to say it."

Another man who although not one of the original organizers of Central was a charter member, affiliating in 1919, was Emil Johansen, who passed away several years ago.

"We never had a financial crisis at Central in the early days because our needs were always carefully anticipated and plans were made to meet them," he recalled. "One time we needed some extra money and everyone was told to think of ways in which it could be earned. Someone got the idea that pictures of our church would be welcomed by those who were affiliated with it — you know, a picture postcard on which the sender could write a line to folks back home, like, 'This is my church.' We had a thousand of them printed, which we sold for five cents each. They went so well that soon we had to have another batch printed. It wasn't much, but it all helped."

Another project was recalled that was far more lucrative than the postcard sale.

"Central soon had an organized men's club which became very active in the affairs of the church. In fact, we became a bit too optimistic and 'overpromised' ourselves. As a group we pledged to pay into the building fund, but other expenses arose and we failed to live up to our promise. Soon we were over $5,000 in arrears, a sizable sum for those days. One evening at a regular meeting we were discussing the distressing matter. Our church was depending upon the money and we had no intention of letting it down. Yet the amount was so large — what could we do?

"Someone suggested that we could secure the services of the Apollo Club for a concert for $500. This club was a highly esteemed local singing group, even as it is today. We decided to sponsor their appearance and set about making arrangements. It was a smashing success. The sum of $6,400 was taken in, with no really heavy expenses. We cleared up our club's arrears — with a little left over."

There were other matters that needed attention, too, for the problems of a new church are many. For some time Central got along without a choir, though it was realized by all that one would have to be organized soon. A men's choir was organized, but it failed to survive more than six months. A permanent, mixed group was needed. The congregation was polled and overwhelming support for such a choir was indicated.

"Some of us met at the Curtis Hotel one evening to talk about it, and all of us present were very much for it. We hired an organist and put her on the regular payroll at $75 a month. Then we also hired a director of music to whom we paid $125 a month. We were in business! At Christmas that first year of the choir we sang Handel's 'Messiah.'"

What Mr. Johansen did not tell was that he was a paper salesman at that time and that he supplied all of the paper needs of the church and the Sunday school. He never submitted a bill.

From the diary of one of the founders, Oliver Prestholdt, loaned to us by his surviving wife, we glean the following comments:

"I think I am fortunate for having been connected at the beginning with the organization of Central Lutheran Church to witness its infant struggles and to enjoy its earliest victories.

"I personally feel that it is proper to record here, that all of the meetings which I attended during the early days of the church were characterized by a fine spirit of unity, good will and a deep desire for the success and advancement of the congregation.

"The problem of providing accommodations for the constant increase in the number of people that came to worship in Central grew daily larger and more complex. What could be done by a small congregation with little or no finances on hand? The amount of cash that had been accumulated was used up in the purchase of the church property. The seating capacity of the church became the number one problem. It became clear that a new sanctuary with a much larger seating capacity must be the solution.

"When I was a member of the Board of Trustees, I suggested that a Committee of Twelve be appointed at large to discuss ways and means of solving our problem. The men selected were: Dr. F. E. Moody, Christ Wangaard, O. L. Loberg, E. H. Sund, O. E. Brecke, C. O. Johnson, O. J. Thorpe, A. M. Hoveland, C. A. Bossen, Dr. Ivar Sivertsen, C. H. Christofferson, and myself. Dr. Stub and C. A. Thiele, our office manager, were ex officio members.

"Many meetings were held at which there were free discussions and many interesting suggestions were proposed. Occasionally the discussion engendered a little heat, but all in good fellowship. The question was: What could this group recommend to the Board of

Trustees that would seem to be, if carried out, a solution to the very pressing need of providing sufficient seating capacity to meet the present and future growth of the congregation? Should the Committee recommend taking down the old church and building a new structure there? Should a new site adjacent to the old church be purchased and build a rather inexpensive auditorium of sufficient capacity, or should the Committee recommend building a church cathedral of a permanent character, large enough to meet the present and future needs of the church? It should be noted that E. H. Sund, the architect, and Dr. Stub persisted in the idea of recommending a new church building. Their ideas prevailed.

"Let us remember that it was not easy for a group of experienced and hardheaded businessmen, whose training in the past had been to meet their bills when they became due, to vote the building of a new church, and they did so with some hesitation. There existed a reluctance to recommend sailing out on an uncharted sea to obligate such a small congregation with an expenditure of $500,000. It looked somewhat visionary, but all the members of the Committee finally joined in approving the idea to go ahead with a new church building. A building committee was appointed and it was decided to have the plans of the new church drawn by Sund & Dunham.

"I was appointed by the Trustees, as a committee of one, to negotiate for the purchase of the land upon which the sanctuary now stands. After many meetings and dickering about the price with Mr. Kunze, vice president of Marquette National Bank, who had been appointed trustee for the heirs of the property, we finally agreed on a price of $24,000.

"I met with Dr. Stub in his office many times. He worried considerably about the finances of the church project. He labored diligently and took in silence, many of the letters of abuse which he received, particularly from pastors, of the failure of the church to make the interest payments on the outstanding bonds. He also received many letters criticizing him for speaking in churches of other denominations, and for associating with clergymen of other faiths. He took his trials and tribulations admirably, and when he passed on, I joined with others to say, 'A great man in Israel has fallen!'"

CHAPTER 4

Vignettes of Recollection

"Doers as well as dreamers."

Many are the interesting accounts that have crept into the records of Central Lutheran Church during its formative years. In a hundred different items, the success story is told.

A "Go to Church" campaign was begun in the late winter of 1920. It was endorsed by the Lutheran Ministers' Federation of Minneapolis and concerned all Lutheran churches of the city. No joint services were held. The whole emphasis was placed on attendance at the church of one's choice. Cards were placed in streetcars; newspaper advertisements were carried; circulars were widely distributed. The campaign was four weeks in length and Central entered into the spirit of the movement wholeheartedly.

Visitors to Central were surprised a few days later to receive a card in the mail. "Thank you for your attendance," it read. "We hope that you were benefited by worshipping at Central. Come again. We shall send you more information about our work. Meanwhile, won't you consider Central to be your church home? The pastor or another member of the congregation will be glad to meet with you at any time. We would like to tell you about our hopes and plans."

There were eight cards in all, for no one card would do for all visitors. To out-of-town visitors or tourists, the card read, "We hope that you arrived home safely and found your loved ones well. When in Minneapolis again, please visit us."

When it became apparent that it would be better for Central to purchase the building that it occupied rather than to continue to rent it, the pastor wrote to his congregation: "The time has come when we should cease to be renters. A day should come when we can say with gratitude, 'This is *our* church.' Let us in God's name decide to move forward. A meeting will be called soon to determine our course. Every member must consider it a sacred duty to be present."

Although at times there was a scarcity of money to carry on the full operation of the church, no phase of its many activities was ever slighted in favor of more pressing needs of the moment. In a letter sent by the church treasurer, Mr. J. F. Field, dated November 19, 1919, attention of the congregation was called to the fact that the church was $1,100 in debt. However, an examination of the treasurer's books revealed that the sum of $411.25 had recently been given to the relief of suffering Poland, devastated by the recent war. Also, $321.75 had been given to mission work. These two sums, if added together would have gone a long way toward wiping out the deficit. Together they totaled more than ten percent of the money needed to carry on the work of the congregation, $6,018.24 having been set aside for that purpose.

Letters to members of the congregation provided a personal touch between the church and the parishioners that was a melding force for good. On November 3, 1920, the pastor wrote: "All of Central's members should consider it a duty to invite to affiliate with us those who need a church home. I pray you, let each one of us make a solemn vow now to obtain at least one new member for our beloved Central, for the Sunday School, the Women's Guild, the Girls' Club and other Central organizations. Do this for God and Central Lutheran Church."

Applicants for membership, when approved, received personal notification by letter from the pastor. He wrote: "I am pleased to inform you that . . . you have been unanimously voted a member of this church by the Board of Deacons."

In March 1921, the letter read, "We have over 500 persons who now attend Central but who are not members. Some of them have attended since Central was organized. Has the time now come to affiliate with us? On our second anniversary we should have a thousand members . . ."

Cautious euphemisms were employed to bring home a point. "It is the privilege of all members of Central to subscribe something toward the support of our church. You have undoubtedly not yet been approached on this matter as our records show that no pledge has been received from you to date."

So effective were the personal contact letters that at the end of three years, only $4,000 remained of the $33,000 cost of the building. The contributions ranged from a low of $25 to $1,000. Pledges ran for a period of five years, the average being $150 to be paid in annual installments of $30 each. This was a pleasing figure for those days when incomes were small.

"We must anticipate future needs," the church officers warned. "We should have electric lights throughout the building; we need painting, inside and out; our church basement should be modernized . . ."

No avenue was left unapproached; no possibility was too small to observe. "If you know of anyone who is not as yet associated with a church, will you let us know?" pleaded the pastor.

Those who pledged were sent sincere Thank You letters "for your support of Central with your prayers, your interest, and your means. The Scriptural suggestion may be found in I Corinthians 16:2. Members should look this up."

Another broad hint followed in another letter, addressed to attenders who were nonmembers. It read in part: "You have been attending Central for some time. This indicates, I hope, that you feel somewhat contented with us. Won't you now consider seriously uniting with us?"

An anticipatory question that led eventually to a new church edifice went out to all members as early as the spring of 1921. "What can we do to provide more room for our Sunday morning audiences?" It was four years later that an exultant communication was sent out. "The great campaign for a new church is on!" A dinner was planned in the church dining room to which all were invited to attend. The cost? Thirty-five cents a plate. In big red letters down the left side of the letter were printed the words, "Do it now for Central!" Six months later the committee in charge was able to say, "We now have $100,000 pledged." A new church building, so badly needed, was assured.

"Dinners at this price are unheard of today," observed a longtime member of Central recently. "I can pinpoint the time when inflation began in our country. It was when church dinners jumped from 35 cents to 50 cents."

It was better to have no cost at all for the dinner than to have even a little in those early days of the church. There were too many who might well stay away entirely if any cost at all were attached to a church gathering that involved food. On August 3, 1921, a Women's Guild outing was held at Dr. Moody's home on Lake Minnetonka. "Take the 9:35 a.m. Great Northern train to Spring Park," read the instructions. "Walk to the Nelson's boat landing. Bring your basket, with food for two meals. Coffee and cream will be furnished free."

There were many events scheduled by the different church organizations; a wiener roast for young people; a picnic for the whole family in Como Park in neighboring St. Paul.

A special appeal was frequently made to the young people of the church. The parents were told, "We are very interested in the young people of the church. We want them to be good, happy, respected young men and women, succeeding in life."

During the second year, a letter was sent to the young girls of the church. It read: "A recent survey shows that fully 500 young women attend Central Lutheran. To foster a spirit of good fellowship among our members and to extend it to young women who are here temporarily, we are organizing a Girls' Club to meet each Monday. Dinner will be served at cost, a short program will be given, and classes will be organized as the demand develops."

The first evening meeting was held on January 10, 1921. The cost of the meal for each participant was 15 cents. Thus began the famous young people's meetings that developed into an integral part of the church's activities.

When the famed St. Olaf Choir was scheduled to appear at Central, a subtle appeal was made to the Lutheran pastors of the Twin Cities to aid Central in its project. "In this letter you will find two complimentary tickets. They are for you to use personally. We would greatly appreciate it if you would read to your congregation the enclosed announcements concerning the choir. Anything that you can do to aid in the success of this project will be appreciated."

Needless to say, in every local Lutheran church that Sunday the fame of the St. Olaf Choir was extolled. Also, it goes without saying that the advertising value of the plan was considerable.

An interesting deviation from the usual run-of-mill money-raising project was carried out by Central in May 1933, when the great depression engulfed the nation. Times were hard and money was scarce. A "Melting Pot" campaign was staged. Based on the example provided in Exodus 35:22, "And they came, both men and women, as many were willing-hearted, and brought bracelets and earrings and tablets, all jewels of gold." An appeal went out on March 6, 1933. It was a strategic time to stress the value of items other than money. President Franklin Roosevelt had just taken office and a bank panic by coincidence had occurred at that moment. All banks were closed by Presidential decree pending a stock-taking and actions to safeguard depositors' funds. Temporarily, almost no money was in circulation.

The appeal from the church offices called for "pieces of gold or silver jewelry, broken or whole, old spectacle frames, watches, trinkets — anything containing precious metal, solid or plated . . ." An envelope was enclosed for the smaller items. The larger ones could be

40

brought to the church or would be picked up by committee members upon request of the donor.

A dinner to inaugurate the campaign was held at the church. The cost per plate was 50 cents.

A charter member, Mrs. Clara Moody will long be remembered for her enthusiastic support of every project and worthwhile endeavor in the church. She was the originator of the Martha Mission and directed its social service program until her death. With a "never-say-die" spirit, she participated wholeheartedly, and encouraged others to follow her leadership. One of the projects of the early days was the publishing of a cookbook that netted $10,000 and was used to purchase the first parsonage. Her name is indelibly imprinted on the records of the church for her dedicated service.

It was on May 1, 1934, that a Fifteenth Anniversary banquet was held at the Leamington Hotel. The occasion was used to honor the completion of Dr. Stub's fifteen years at Central as well as to observe the fifteenth anniversary of the birth of the church. A welcome was extended by the president of the congregation who then introduced the master of ceremonies. Then followed *ten* speakers, all ministers holding the D. D. degree. There is no record of the hour at which the session ended, but one can well imagine that twelve speakers would naturally consume a considerable amount of time. At the very end of the program came the thirteenth and final talk of the evening, a response by Dr. Stub.

One wonders today, when dinners seldom cost less than $5.00 and usually are more than that, what kind of meal could be served for the 75-cent fee of that evening. A look at the menu indicates that a full meal was served, beginning with cream of asparagus soup, the meat course, consisting of braised beef tenderloin. Vegetables, rolls, and a salad were included; it all being topped off with cake and coffee. Times have changed.

The difficult years of the depression era were reflected in the life of Central Lutheran in many ways. In the pastor's letter to the parents of the 1930 confirmands, he observed: "The cost of the white robes is $1.00 for rental, cleaning, etc. If any parent cannot afford the $1.00, give us 50 cents or whatever you can afford to give. We will take care of the rest . . ."

CHAPTER 5

Service to Others

"The Miracle Church of America" — Paul Douglas.

The founders of Central Church built well. Upon the foundations which they so carefully laid, the super-structure of one of America's most successful churches was established.

Other pastors of comparable downtown churches watched the progress of Central with admiration. Prominent in church circles at the time was Dr. Roy L. Smith, pastor of Simpson Methodist Episcopal Church of Minneapolis, and well known nationally as a syndicated columnist of "sentence sermons." In a letter to Dr. Stub, he wrote: "I have watched the work of the downtown churches with more than ordinary interest. When I say that the work of Central Lutheran Church, and the pastorate that you have so wonderfully directed, are a source of constant admiration and amazement as well as inspiration to me, you will understand that I am not speaking mere empty words. I know of nothing equal to your success in all America."

Paul Douglas, the nationally known expert of "City Churches," said of Central in 1925: "The miracle church in America. The outstanding example and demonstration of a deliberately adapted church, meeting the needs of the community."

Pastor Stub himself stated the underlying philosophy that had guided the church under his direction to such heights. He said, "Central Lutheran Church, being a downtown church, and situated as it is, must be open every hour of the day, seven days a week. Naturally, its primary purpose is that of preaching the Gospel of our crucified Lord. But I have no patience with the philosophy which divides life into two spheres — the secular and the spiritual. Paul speaks of glorifying God by presenting our bodies as living sacrifices. Therefore, I believe that every phase and activity of life can and should be sanctified and dedicated to the services of the Lord." He set the pattern for Central to be known as the servant church, to counsel and help people regardless of race, color, or creed.

This was the stated philosophy of the man who guided the destinies of Central Lutheran for half the period of its first fifty years of existence. It is a belief so fundamental that the edifice which was built upon it has remained strong and impregnable against the onslaughts of modern idealogies.

In order to put his beliefs into practical usage, Pastor Stub formulated a working program that was designed to achieve the ends that he so patiently sought. No phase of activity was neglected; no group was too small to be included; no person was too young or too old to profit from it. At the end of five years, an analysis was made of the program and its success, item by item and phase by phase. Included in it were such integral parts of the church's activities as these:

The Sunday School — Pastor Stub regarded the Sunday School as the great teaching missionary agency of Central Lutheran Church. It was his stated ambition to make the Sunday School function all through the life of the people of his church. Five years after the church was founded, the names of two hundred and fifty children were included on the Cradle Roll, the majority of whom came from unchurched homes in the immediate vicinity of the church. In order to provide the greatest possible amount of individual attention to each child, the pupil-teacher ratio was set at a low ten to one; that is, each Sunday School teacher had only ten children assigned to her care, according to the author of this book who served as General Superintendent from 1924 to 1939.

It is interesting that this desirable condition has been maintained through the years, and approximately the same ratio prevails today. As a part of the program, each teacher visited her pupils in their homes several times a year. On their birthdays they were always remembered. On special occasions the parents were invited to attend the Sunday School classes, and sometimes both parents and children attended special exercises together. There was a carefully worked out curriculum which led the pupils upward year by year until confirmation time was reached. Nor did their Sunday School experiences end on the day of confirmation. Then came enrollment in a special class which was followed by membership in the Young People's League.

"Every age and condition of our members need and have organized attention," said Pastor Stub. "We are not concerned merely with the children and young people of our own members. We are concerned with the hundreds and thousands of our faith who have no church connection. Their spiritual — and other — needs are always on our minds."

The Fireside Hour — When Central Church was first organized, a meeting of a few of the members was called on the first Sunday afternoon after Easter in order that the newly installed pastor might meet some of the members and friends of the church. These meetings became a regular feature of the church, continuing year after year under the name of the Fireside Hour. The majority who attended these meetings were not regular members of the congregation; they were students, housemaids, and others who were unable to attend the regular Sunday morning services. This was another area of activity to render a service to people outside of the regular membership.

The purpose developed into one of providing activities such as might be observed in any Christian home on a late Sunday afternoon. These meetings were simple in format. At 4:30 the Olson three-piece string ensemble played appropriate music, followed by a half hour spent in singing hymns, after which a short program was given, varied in nature. Following this, a simple lunch was served, care being taken that no one was ever burdened with the preparation of refreshments. It was the kind that anyone might pick up in his own home without asking the mother to prepare it for him.

It was a source of gratification to the sponsors of the Fireside Hour to have so many young people attend, men and women who had no real home in the city and who found in these meetings the companionship which they needed. Many in attendance remained for the Sunday evening services. Often there were five or even six hundred persons in attendance, and when one Sunday afternoon more than seven hundred people gathered together, the joy of the pastor and his helpers was great.

Now they felt that one of their most sought-after objectives was being realized.

"These meetings meant that much time and energy had to be spent by those who were responsible for them, but they were fulfilling the ideal of Central to be of service and to meet every need as it arose," said Pastor Stub.

(Because the Fireside Hour had served its purpose, due to changing conditions it was discontinued during the later half of Dr. Hjortland's pastorate.)

The Women's Guild — This organization began humbly, true to the origin of Central itself, with only a few members forming the charter group in May 1919. It, too, grew in numbers as did the other organizations of the church, and when a count was taken at the end of the first five years, it was found that more than three hundred women were affiliated.

Ten circles were included in the Guild. Each of the circles was assigned a month during which it was made responsible for all of the activities that fell within its month. They paid for the orchestra that led the church "sings," and took charge of the lunches that were served during the Sunday afternoon Fireside Hour. Each circle divided the responsibilities among its approximately thirty members. A committee that represented the Guild arranged for programs which were given free of charge in the church. Some of the city's outstanding musicians gave their services free of charge. These programs were extremely popular with the congregation and they played an integral part in melding the group into one dynamic force.

The Girls' Club — Because of the mobile nature of the community in which Central Church was located, it was regarded as essential that there be a program that would bring into active participation the young people who came to the city for employment. One of the groups organized for this purpose was the Girls' Club.

This group met every Monday evening from September through May. Beginning with but a small number of members, its roster grew when, largely by word of mouth, its function became known throughout the city. By the time five years had passed, more than three hundred girls were enrolled in its program, though it was not unusual to have five hundred or even more present at Monday evening sessions. The attendance was especially gratifying at the special meetings such as at Thanksgiving time or at the St. Valentine's Day party. It was an organization that from the very beginning was managed by the girls themselves.

The worth of the Girls' Club was built about a program of activities, each one included because of an interest on the part of some of the members.

Classes that proved popular were Bible Study, Book Reviews, Expression, Basketry, Needlework, Dressmaking, Millinery, China Painting, Ukelele Playing, French, and òthers. Competent instructors were located for each class, their services being volunteered. Therefore the cost to each of the girls was almost negligible. Dinner was served at a nominal cost preceding each meeting. An extension division was organized and hundreds of calls were made on girls living in the congested area of the city to acquaint them with the program.

Once each year the Girls' Club held a public display of articles that they had made in the classes. Hundreds of items were included in the demonstration of their ability, such as dresses, lingerie, painted china, lamp shades, needlework, and basketry, to mention but a few.

(This club was active for another ten years after which the group was disbanded.)

The Men's Club — If there was a girls' club available at the church, of course there had to be a men's club also. Like the girls, the men met once a month, though because of the functions served by the numerous committees, its activities were more in evidence about the church throughout the entire month.

The club, five years after its founding, had a membership of one hundred and fifty, many of whom were nonmembers of Central Lutheran. It affiliated with the Lutheran Brotherhood of America as well as with the local Hennepin County Federation. Among its members were many young men who found in the club the associations which they missed so much because of their absence from home.

(The Men's Club was continued as an active organization until 1964.)

The Young People's League — When the Young People's League was in the process of being organized, Dr. Stub said, "This league will not exist merely for the purpose of providing a home for the youth who are members of the church. The same vision of service to others that we have in our other organizations will be present in this one also."

Every Wednesday evening the young people met at the church, often more than five hundred being present. The meetings were devotional, inspirational and social in purpose. On special occasions events were held which attracted young people from all sections of the city, such as the annual spring picnic, which was held in one of the city's parks. The Christmas party was unique.

"I shall never forget the Christmas party held last year," recalled Pastor Stub. "All of the lights were turned off except those illuminating the Christmas trees as the hundreds of young people present sang their favorite hymns and carols that they had sung and loved since childhood days. Many of those present were away from home, some of them for the first time, and their thoughts were back there with their families and friends that evening."

(A complete reorganization of youth activities were made in later years with the establishment of several youth organizations to meet the challenges of a new era.)

Nurses' Clubs — One of the truly unique groups sponsored by Central Church was the Nurses' Club. There were in the city hundreds of young women taking nurses' training at the various hospitals, and many others who had finished their training and were already registered nurses. This club was organized to bring together as many of these girls as possible, attracted together because of similar interests. It was open to all, irrespective of church affiliation. It was with some pride that the sponsors noted in 1925 that twenty-one hospitals were represented by member nurses.

(Later, nurses were absorbed into several organizations that provided a well-balanced program.)

Teachers' Club — Each year new teachers were needed to fill vacant classroom positions in the city. Many of these men and women were recruited from the smaller towns of the state. Like the nurses and others new to the city, they sought companionship and social activities outside of their immediate sphere of activity. The Teachers' Club was organized to bring together members of this profession, both men and women. It attracted many persons to its meetings where a felt need was met.

(Likewise, teachers later became members in the several organizations more closely aligned to their interests.)

Boys' and Girls' Clubs — The younger members of the congregation and the community were not neglected at Central. Various clubs catered to their interests. One of the popular groups was the Boy Scout Troop No. 55 which was sponsored by the Men's Club. It was affiliated with the Minneapolis Scout organization and was organized according to its procedure. A Scout Troop Committee of the Men's Club was the group's overseer. The Scouts met every week at the church under the leadership of a scoutmaster selected by the committee.

There was also a Girl Scout troop at Central, organized on lines similar to those of the boys' group. It, too, met each week at the church and carried on an interesting program of activities. The large number of both boys and girls belonging to the Scout organizations attested to their worth.

Another group of younger girls called itself the Busy Bees. It was composed of girls as young as six years of age. At the meetings of the group, the members were taught not only such practical arts as sewing and raffia work, but also the proper methods of conducting a meeting. Their motto was "Service to Others" and to put it into practical effect, they supported a native missionary in China. At Christmastime they collected gifts and food which were presented to the needy of the city.

General Activities — It was only natural that the work done at Central should draw heavily upon its resources and interests in relation to the less fortunate. A department of the Women's Guild, known as the Missionary Circle, later the Martha Mission, met every other Wednesday of the month and spent the entire day sewing garments and comforters for the needy. Thirty sewing machines were used by the members in this valuable activity. Thousands of garments of all kinds were prepared and distributed each year. The recipients were selected by the parish sister, who was a trained deaconess.

Another group of women met in the church every week to distribute clothing from the well-stocked storeroom. The number of families who were made more comfortable through this activity on the part of the women of the church is legion. It must be remembered that when Central Lutheran Church was young, there were not available to needy families the funds that are now distributed so freely by governmental agencies. Those in need had to rely largely upon private organizations to augment their wants.

The same spirit which motivated the women to take action to help the less fortunate was found also among the Sunday School classes. Although their concern was ever-present, it was especially around Christmastime that it was put into greater action. Then each class was made responsible for meeting the needs of one or more families, and many were the tales that were told, after the Christmas season had ended, of the happiness that had been brought into the lives of others because of their concern. The Boy Scout and Girl Scout troops also took an active part in this type of activity, guided by the watchword of their church, "Service to Others."

Pastor Stub was a psychologist as well as a laborer in the field. He understood people and knew well the emotions whicn guided their actions. He knew that there were many people with special problems who could be reached only if an opportunity were provided for them to discuss their problems privately. He let it be known that he would be in his office at the church during regular hours and so would the parish sister. Individuals were encouraged to come to the church during these hours to discuss their problems freely. Few, indeed, were the days that passed without someone coming for help or counsel to the pastor or the parish sister.

A strong missionary and benevolence program was initiated at Central right from the start. It was recognized that while the need for foreign missionary service was great, there was also a need right within the confines of the area served by the church, for immediate aid. Every year large sums of money were spent for food, clothing, medicine and other needed items. There were also many individuals as well as other organizations and groups within the church which contributed money for such purposes. All of the distribution of these monies and materials came under the jurisdiction of the parish deaconess, Sister Marie. The extent of the distribution of benevolences during this period as well as during the later life of the church will never be known, for much of it was done quietly and without official record. There was never a thought of "What does this mean for me?"

but always the goal of service to others was the guiding spirit. The Biblical injunction that "It is more blessed to give than to receive" was seldom more faithfully adhered to.

The work of the parish sister became so demanding that it was soon apparent that it could not be effectively done without the aid of an automobile. One was accordingly purchased for her use and the work of distribution was made easier and more complete. One of the early members of the church who took an active part in this phase of the church's work estimated that the number of calls made by the parish sister increased fourfold after she was provided with an automobile.

One of the obligations that was taken very seriously by the workers within the church was that of calling upon the sick. A list was kept up to date at all times and a record kept of the calls made. When a Sunday School child was absent for two successive Sundays, the home was visited to determine the reason for the absence. Since the community in which Central is located was, and still is, an area of great mobility, the turnover in membership both in the church and in its organizations was large. Many families moved into the neighborhood, made a brief stay, and moved on. Where did they go? Often no one knew. All too frequently, it is probable that no one cared. Central did its best to serve them during their stay and had to be content with that being well done, but it hoped that in doing this it would instill in their hearts a better understanding of the meaning of Christian service to others.

In these and other ways did Central Lutheran Church during its formative years establish a program of service that was as solid as the Rock upon which the Christian church had been built. Pastor Stub had laid the foundation for this program during his initial talks with the little congregation in 1919. It was to be an open-door church for everyone, he had said. It was not to be a church that served a select group only, this being the members of the congregation and no others. While the entire program that was being developed was built around the Christian doctrine as it was enunciated from the pulpit, it was by no means confined to the public worship hour. From the pulpit it expanded in ever-widening circles, like the ripples on a pond when a stone is thrown into the water. So large were the crowds that came to worship at Central on Sunday mornings that it early became necessary to hold three services on two Sundays of each month.

For its 11 o'clock service on Easter Sunday, 1923, Central rented the Lyceum Auditorium. Twenty minutes before eleven the doors of the auditorium were closed. There were 3,000 people inside, and between 1,200 and 1,800 were outside seeking admission. Besides, some 600 people who did not know that the meeting place had been changed met in the church. About 500 were present at the sunrise service that same Sunday.

Easter Sunday, 1924, Central was unable to rent the Lyceum Auditorium so five services were held in the church, with a total attendance of 6,000. Easter Sunday, 1925, three services were held in the church, with a total attendance of 4,200.

As the end of the sixth year of Central's active life approached, it became apparent that under almost no conceivable circumstance could all of the potential worshippers be accommodated on Easter Sunday morning. The pastor and deacons debated the matter and decided to do something that probably had never been done in Minneapolis before. Service would be held not in the church sanctuary, but in the largest building available in the city — the Armory, located on the parade grounds, a mile or so to the west of Central. Plans were made accordingly.

The day arrived and with it the throngs, eager to take part in a worship service that was to be regarded as one of the most thrilling church gatherings in the history of the city.

A large platform had been built, seventy-five feet long, especially for this service. It was a veritable garden of lilies and other flowers and plants, encircling a large cross. Two hundred persons in addition to the choir were seated upon it. At 10:30 a.m., a full half hour before the service was to begin, the building had been filled to capacity. There were 5,800 seats in the auditorium, each one occupied. Standing in the aisles and occupying every available bit of other space were over 2,000 more people. An overflow crowd of 2,000 more was gathered outside.

Probably never before in the history of Minneapolis had so many people assembled for an Easter service. Certainly it was one of the best-attended Easter services in the nation that day. The eloquent sermon preached by Dr. Stub, whose subject was, "How Much Do You Believe in God?" was the reward of the 10,000 for being present that day.

Dr. Stub had once said: "This church must strive to be a real church home for people of all conditions and ages. It must teem with activity. Its doors must be open to welcome all, irrespective of antecedents or social position. It must be "our Father's house" where all can

The completed Sanctuary, 1927

The interior of the Sanctuary

The Baptismal Chapel

The Marriage Chapel

The Organ

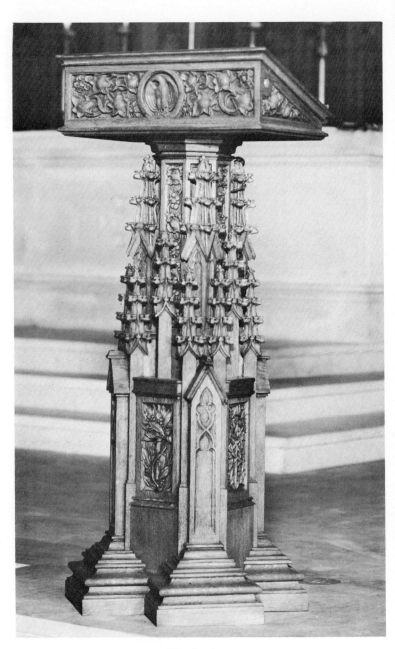

The Lectern

The Pulpit

The Chancel for an Easter Service

feel at home. In other words, the church does not exist so much for its members as for the opportunity that it gives them to serve the common Lord."

As he viewed the half decade of Central's existence from the vantage point of the mid-1920's, he and his workers could well feel that this objective was being achieved. While Pastor Stub was giving the credit for the success of Central to the blessing of God and the hard work of this congregation, they were saying of him, "Well done, thou good and faithful servant." The results of his labors have been felt through the years, even to this day.

CHAPTER 6

A Cathedral Is Built

"To God Alone the Glory."

The crowded church building of the newly organized congregation known as Central Lutheran on Easter Sunday, April 20, 1919, was an omen of things to come. Only the Sunday before had Pastor Stub been installed as the church's first minister. If the edifice was filled to capacity at the first worship service after the installation of the newly called pastor, what would the future bring?

As time went on, events proved the truth of the Easter morning prediction. Sunday after Sunday the auditorium of the church was filled to overflowing. On special occasions, all of the people who sought entrance to Central could not be admitted, many being turned away. Every worship service was a testimonial to the faith that the founders had in their experiment. Now they knew that it had the blessing of God, whose structure it was.

During the first year that the old Baptist Central Church housed the Central Lutheran congregation, the structure was rented. However, it was apparent from the first that ownership should be acquired, and accordingly on February 26, 1920, the congregation unanimously authorized the Board of Trustees to purchase the building and the three lots on which it stood, at the corner of Grant Street and Fourth Avenue South. The price agreed upon was $33,000.

Two years later, in order to increase the seating capacity of the building, the wall between the auditorium and the Sunday School quarters was removed. However, this was but an expedient. The membership had grown phenomenally, and even with this increased capacity, the room did not meet the needs of the church. Clearly something had to be done, for each week people were being turned away from divine services.

Before another year went by the initial steps were taken that led eventually to a solution to the problem in the form of a new church edifice. At the annual meeting of the congregation in 1923, the pastor was authorized to appoint a Committee of Twelve which was instructed to deliberate carefully upon the vexing question of what could be done toward affecting an equitable solution to the problem. During the course of their deliberations, the advice of knowledgeable persons was sought; architects, engineers and contractors contributing to the discussions. The first question to be considered was, "Is it feasible to remodel or enlarge the existing structure?" It had been built in the year 1883, and was in serviceable condition, but it was the opinion of those whose advice was sought that this could not be done and yet retain proper beauty of design and practicality of function. The inevitable conclusion was reached that nothing short of an entirely new structure would provide a satisfactory solution to the problem.

Meanwhile, the church officials from time to time rented the Lyceum Auditorium, several blocks away, and 1925 witnessed the thrilling spectacle of 10,000 people seeking entry to the Armory on Easter morning. Clearly there was needed a building that would seat at least 3,000 persons. Nothing less than this would be satisfactory.

At the annual meeting of the congregation of Central Lutheran Church, held on January 12, 1925, there was a prolonged discussion about the wisdom of building a sanctuary. When it was evident that there would be opposition for making an immediate decision to proceed with such plans because of the prospect of a financial load beyond the capacity of the small membership, Dr. Stub arose to exhort the members to have faith in their future.

"We have witnessed during the last five years," said Dr. Stub, "the overwhelming support of our missionary effort in the heart of Minneapolis. We cannot disappoint the thousands of people we are destined to serve in the future. I urge you to authorize the Board of Trustees to proceed with plans to build a new church as proposed by the Committee of Twelve. If you wish to discuss this task without my presence, I will retire to another room."

There was further discussion until one member proposed that "we increase Dr. Stub's salary by $500." It was hoped that the pastor would withdraw his request until later when the church was in a better financial position. When Dr. Stub was called back into the meeting and informed of the salary increase, his response was positive:

"I refuse to accept it. Since I came to Central I have had several calls from other Lutheran churches at a much larger salary, but I have returned the calls because I believe that I am needed here." And then he declared decisively: "I have only one life to live and that life is dedicated to the future growth of Central."

That settled the matter. The fainthearted members took renewed courage, and two resolutions were passed. The first one authorized the church to conduct a campaign to raise the necessary funds to finance the erection of a new church. The second gave the Board of Trustees the right to acquire additional property on which to build the new structure, if events proved the necessity of so doing. The next month, at a special meeting of the congregation, legal technicalities were properly disposed of relating to the plans under consideration. The way was now cleared for the campaign for funds to begin.

A bond-selling organization was engaged to conduct a sale of mortgage bonds throughout the communities of the Northwest. So well known had the phenomenal growth of Central become among the Lutheran churches in this five-state area, that the first issue of first mortgage bonds was oversubscribed and within a month $375,000 worth of bonds had been sold. The Board was urged to then offer second mortgage bonds, and another $200,000 was subscribed within the next month.

Why not build a great cathedral patterned after old-world architecture? Another issue of notes was offered and quickly sold. The final result was that $675,000 worth of securities were sold and the money was available to proceed with building plans.

It now became necessary for members of the church to pledge their financial support to underwrite the financing for the new building. As a result of the campaign, sufficient pledges backed by promissory notes were raised to cover the entire amount of $675,000, payable over a period of years. Meanwhile, properties necessary for the construction of the new church home were being acquired, for it was the intention of the congregation not only to build a new structure, but to retain the one that they already possessed. By midsummer an architect had been hired to draw up suitable plans and specifications. Clearly the plans to provide a new church home were progressing rapidly.

It was on the seventh Sunday after Trinity, on July 18, 1926, that the congregation proceeded out to the old church in solemn procession to witness the breaking of ground on the new site, all in the name of the Triune God. The people's dream of a new church home was about to be realized. Work began at once.

On the Sunday after Thanksgiving, November 28, 1926, services were held at Central Lutheran and the cornerstone of the new church was laid. It was to be a magnificent structure, worthy of the ideals upon which it was founded. It would be in truth a temple, a cathedral church, to be dedicated to the cause of service in the name of God. It was soon to be recognized as the threshold of Lutheranism in Minneapolis. On the cornerstone were inscribed in Latin the words, "To God alone the glory."

Taking part in the ceremony was the venerable father of Pastor Stub, long a servant in the Lord's vineyard. Seven years before this date he had participated in the installation of his son as pastor of this same church. What magnificent happenings he had witnessed since that day! Now he proudly took part in the laying of the cornerstone of the new cathedral of worship to which thousands of people would flock weekly to hear his son preach the Gospel of Jesus Christ. Truly, his son and the church that he served had been richly blessed since that Palm Sunday morning just seven years before.

The first worship service in the new edifice was an event that was looked forward to for many months. It was the dream of the founders from the very beginning of their venture that someday a magnificent new church structure would rise from the spot where the old building stood. First, their experiment would have to prove its worth. Only then could they go forth into broadened fields. Now that day had come!

Fittingly, it was on the church's most joyous festival day that the first service was held in the new structure. Christmas Day in 1927 fell on a Sunday and it was then that the pastor and the officials of the church decided that the new building should first be used. True, it was not as yet fully completed, but that would come in short time. It was sufficient that the building was complete enough to make worshipping possible.

It was a magnificent edifice that the Christmas Day worshippers entered that morning. It stood at the crossroads in the heart of the metropolis of the Midwest, a great Gothic cathedral, a storied structure of stone, classic in outline, beautiful in form, a fitting monument to the faith of its founders. It was a mighty citadel that seemed to grow from the very ground. Its massive walls led the eyes of the approaching worshippers onward and upward, past storied windows and a triple-terraced effect, to the steeply pitched roof, up to the copper fleche with its gargoyles, to the crown of the temple, a golden cross.

Built of Indiana limestone, it was the first building in this part of America to be constructed of this material. The stone was taken from the quarries without any attempt at selection as to color or texture. It was tiered in "random ashlar," using stones of five different sizes, with no attempt to make it appear coursed. The result was a pleasing wall of soft variety.

The 175-foot tower, an architectural masterpiece, was not completed on that day, and yet remains a project of the future. The small, slender spire above the intersection of the nave and transepts was made entirely of copper. True to its Gothic type, it was full of details, pinnacles and gargoyles. The slender, graceful cross was made of brass while the stone cross at the top of the front gable was massive, standing twelve feet high and weighing one and a half tons. To a viewer approaching the building it appeared like a cathedral of the old world.

The worshippers that cold Christmas morning, having looked in wonder at the great structure as they approached it, now entered the building. If the outside of the church was impressive, the interior was breathtaking. The entranceway itself, though plain, was true Gothic. At the top of the arch was a dove, symbolic of the spirit of God. As one entered the church, the sense of size and beauty was strong.

The first floor, seating 1,750 people, was almost square. At the front of the huge room stood the altar, dominating the church. The prime purpose of the sanctuary was to accentuate the altar. The sanctuary platform rose five steps from the main floor. Near the outside edge was the communion rail at which seventy people could kneel at one time. The altar, severely plain, was made of huge slabs of Colfax sandstone. Upon it were placed six massive bronze candlesticks, three on each side of the plain bronze cross. The six candles, in their silent way, reminded viewers of the six hours that the Savior hung upon the cross. The plain cross was symbolical of the finished redemption. In this manner were those who looked upon it reminded of the words spoken by Christ as he bowed his head and said, "It is finished."

The second floor or gallery, seating about 1500 people, gave promise of the beautiful true cross shape of the clerestory, which determined the architectural character of the building. As is true of such a Gothic building, the eyes of the beholders unconsciously traveled upward to the arched and vaulted ceiling, which was tiled in five different shades of brown, tan, and gray, which predominated the others. More than a dozen Gothic patterns in gold helped to brighten the ceiling, creating an impression of life. The walls were decorated in old gold.

The graceful, fluted pillars were made of Caen stone. At the spring of the arch they branched out into ribs which joined at the top of the ceilings. The effect was that of an aisle of great trees on both sides of a road, the branches reaching out for each other and knitting together over the center.

The gallery panels and railings facing three sides of the building, joining into the organ screens and finally completing the chancel, were all of wood. The details were typically Gothic. Particularly noticeable were the four organ screens with their gold pipes, the tracery work and the pinnacles. The woodwork was finished in a way that brought out the grain of the wood, yet at the same time it was soft and restful like the woods in the age-old cathedrals of Europe.

The pulpit and the lectern, viewed at leisure by the assembled congregation, were both objects that caught the attention. They were the two most elaborate furnishings of the sanctuary. Each one was richly handcarved in Gothic style. The five faces of the pulpit carried the symbolical shields of the four evangelists, two on each side of the center panel with its symbolism of the victorious Lamb of God. Carved into the frieze near the top of the panel were the words: "Go ye therefore into all the world and preach the Gospel to every creature."

The lectern, finished in the same color as the wood of the church and the pulpit, carried such varied symbols as the Gospel eagle, the grapevine, and that of the Trinity.

The choir pews, seating eighty persons, were placed back of the altar, across the sanctuary in four rows, terraced up from the platform. In this manner were symmetry and grace maintained in the design of the church.

On each side of the sanctuary there was a small chapel, raised several steps above the main floor and separated from the rest of the building by hand-carved wood pillars and tracery. The chapel on the right was designed to be used as the baptistery. The one on the left contained a small sanctuary platform with a wrought iron communion rail and a small oak altar. This chapel was destined to be used for weddings and communions. Upon its altar was placed the cross and the candelabra which had been used in the old building.

Beautiful cathedral windows graced the auditorium. In the lower windows showing on the side aisles were representatives of the great countries which had embraced the faith of Martin Luther since the Reformation, arranged in the chronological order of their conversion. Each country was represented by its national shield mounted by a crown, back of which was displayed the cross of the Reformation. Included were: Germany, Saxony, Sweden, Finland, Denmark, Norway, Iceland, Russia, Holland, and Switzerland on the one side of the church. On the opposite side were: France, England, Poland, Scotland, Canada, and America. The flags of these countries were displayed above the balconies on both sides.

Thus did the beautiful new edifice stand on Christmas Day in the year 1927, opening wide its doors to all who cared to enter.

On Palm Sunday, April 1, 1928, the new church was dedicated. Present and participating in the inspiring services that day was the Right Rev. H. G. Stub, father of the pastor, who had taken part officially at the installation of his son as pastor of Old Central and also at the laying of the cornerstone of the new building. What wonders his eyes had witnessed, as performed by his illustrious son. On this spring day he felt that surely his life was complete, for there was nothing more than his dedicated heart could desire. Truly, the years' memories lay lightly on his mind.

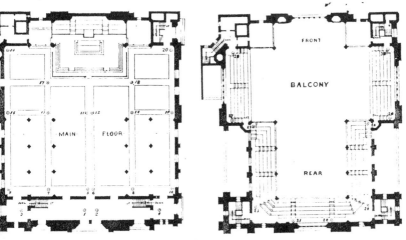

Floor Plans (*The numbered places indicate the stations for the thirty ushers*)

CHAPTER 7

Central's First Fifteen Years

"This is the Lord's doing. It is marvelous in our eyes." — Psalms 118:23

There were troubles and weaknesses in the Lutheran church sixty years ago that were frequently emphasized by the character of the times. This was particularly true in the large cities. It was a time of great population mobility, accentuated by the war. Millions of young men and women joined the military service, willingly or otherwise, and were transported to places far from home. Several million of them were sent overseas. The safety of home was replaced by the dangers of the battlefield. Many who did not become a part of the military forces left home to seek jobs elsewhere, often in war-supply plants in or near the cities. There they were absorbed in the hectic life of the metropolitan areas, finding little resemblance between it and the life that they had previously known.

Dr. Stub's wartime experiences had prepared him well for the leadership role that he assumed at Central Lutheran. Through his travels to the training camps all over America, he had become acquainted firsthand with conditions as they existed. He was troubled by what he saw.

"I came to know many hundreds of men personally," he said. "I realized ever more keenly the weaknesses of our church, especially in the large cities. It was with a sense of shock that I observed our youth failing to find for themselves a church home in the cities, except those who located in the more comfortable and well-established home neighborhoods. In city after city I was shown sites where once Lutheran congregations had flourished, but which had been unable to maintain themselves where now the rush of city life prevailed.

"Many people, especially the younger generation, were being estranged from their former church contacts; countless Lutheran young people were affiliating with churches of other denominations for the simple reason that there was unavailable a church of their own denomination nearby. When I thought of the faithful work of our rural and small-town pastors, going for naught once their members went to the large cities, I knew that there was much to be done. Was our church — the historic church of the great Reformation — to be impotently unable to meet the problems presented at the heart of our great cities? I longed to accept the challenge!"

It was this spirit, burning in the heart of a great minister, that through him permeated the founders of Central Lutheran and made it a great church. They were united in their goal; they worked with a burning purpose. The petty schisms that infect like a cancer the congregations of some churches were lacking at Central. Selflessness was found where selfishness too often flourishes; unity of purpose was the rule rather than recognition of individual effort. That is why Central became a great impelling force instead of just another metropolitan church.

There were other forces that worked in behalf of the founders of Central Lutheran during its formative years. Pastor Stub did not come as an unknown to head the new church. One of the founders and he were boyhood friends; a young couple and he were friends during seminary days; another congregation member had been a boyhood acquaintance of his brother; several others he had known since childhood. The list could be lengthened; each name added another strong link to the chain that was binding the members of the group together. There were few weaknesses, but many were the strengths of the founding family. Working as a united force, they recognized no limits to their accomplishments.

As the years went by, Dr. Stub asked himself, "Would the men who organized Central have the courage to do so again? Would they have begun this work if they had realized what it would mean in terms of work, sacrifices and anxieties? They were only a handful — but so were Christ's disciples when they set out on their mission of spreading the new faith. Could this new church, so different in concept from what we were accustomed, succeed? There were many who prophesied failure. It took great courage to succeed."

On the tenth anniversary of the founding of Central Church, a communication was handed to Pastor Stub. It was hand-written and signed by the officers of the church, the chairmen of boards and committees, and the presidents of the church's auxiliaries. It read: "Ten of the best years of your life have been given to the service of God as the beloved pastor of Central Lutheran. With humble, grateful hearts we thank our Heavenly Father for the blessings of these wonderful years and unite in praying that grace and peace be multiplied unto you through the knowledge of God and of Jesus Christ."

Written a year after the dedication of the new church, it was framed and hung on the wall of the pastor's study, where it remained until his death.

The next year, tragedy came to the church when Aleda Stub, wife of the pastor, died. She had been a strong force during all the formative years and her presence was sadly missed.

When Central Church was planned eleven years previously, two smaller chapels had been designed, one on either side of the great main altar. The one on the left had come to be known as the Marriage Chapel because of the many marriages that were solemnized there. The other chapel was set aside as a baptistery. Hundreds of little children and many adults were covenanted with God through holy baptism in this room.

Many of Aleda Stub's friends wished to leave some memorial to her memory in the church in which she worked so faithfully. After much deliberation it was decided that no more suitable memorial was available than the Memorial Chapel. The room was completely renovated, with a new grill extending across the back of the brocade-covered altar. An original lighting system brought out anew the beauty of the room. On the stone wall was placed a bronze tablet with these words on it: *Aleda Hooverson Stub Memorial Chapel.* In this manner the many friends who loved her left a fitting reminder of one who filled a large niche in the early history of Central Lutheran.

It was in 1930 that Aleda Stub died. A year later the venerable Rev. H. G. Stub, father of the pastor, also passed away. He had, during his long lifetime of more than four score years, labored hard for his beloved church. He had played an integral part in the founding and firm establishment of Central. In accordance with his expressed wishes, he was laid to rest from this church. Thus within the space of a year, death came to claim two members of Central who would be sadly missed in the years to come.

With the coming of the 1930's, new troubles arose for Central Lutheran which for several years threatened to engulf it and to end its existence. They came with the economic depression which swept the country during that decade. The new edifice had hardly been completed before disturbing rumors came from the East of hard times coming to end the decade and a half of affluence. World War I had ushered in a new era. The old days were gone, the so-called "horse and buggy" era. With the automobile and the war came more jobs, better living conditions, and restlessness. A minor recession had been experienced in the early '20's, but it had proved to be short lived. The years that followed had been good ones and money was spent freely. Good times were here and there were many more wonderful years to come, so everyone believed.

The year 1929 brought the nation back to realism. The boom was over; belts had to be tightened and acquaintance made with a new word — austerity. People out of jobs had no money to spend and there was no paternalistic Federal government to provide limitless funds from its coffers. Central Lutheran was heavily in debt, owing more than $600,000 on its new building. As the '30's progressed, matters worsened, eventually coming to the point where the interest on the debt

72

exceeded the year's income. It appeared that only insolvency and repudiation of the debt would provide a solution to the problem.

During these hard years, the loyalty of the members was like a balm to the tired hearts of the pastor and officers. What was done was done for others; "service" remained the watchword of the workers.

The difficult years passed. On the fifteenth anniversary, Pastor Stub was able to say in heartfelt tones, "We lift our hearts to God in humble gratitude. This is the Lord's doing."

On Easter day, 1934, the church was filled to capacity. Over a thousand more people came to worship at Central that day than all of the Minneapolis churches of its synod could have contained in 1919 even if they had been filled to capacity twice over. Because of Central there had been an advance in Lutheranism in Minneapolis during the fifteen years which was, indeed, remarkable. It is doubtful if there was then a city in America where anything comparable to Central's progress could be found. The inspiration that it provided could not be fully realized except through a careful review of church history in the city since 1919.

The encouragement and sympathetic understanding which the pastor and officers received from people outside of their church were a source of much comfort to Central's leadership during these years. One of the men who marveled at this church's progress was Dr. Gerberding, one of the true founders of English Lutheranism in the Northwest. In 1928, he wrote to Dr. Stub, "I like Central Lutheran Church. It is vigorously, courageously attacking the downtown problem. It is soundly Lutheran. It is an abiding encouragement to every English Lutheran minister in the Northwest. I glory in Central Church. I rejoice in and thank God for its rising cathedral."

Accompanying his letter was a check for $25, the final payment on the $100 pledge that he had voluntarily made to Central's building fund. Three days later he was killed by a hit-run driver in Virginia.

On the fifteenth anniversary, Dr. Stub wrote: "Time and again there has been accomplished for us what has seemed like a miracle. More than once it has appeared as if the door was closed upon some plan or hope, but suddenly it was opened for us. It was not because of anything that we deserved, but only because God has wanted Central to be here. As long as He needs us, He will provide the opportunity, the ability and the strength. In God's name, let us go forward as He leads us, committing our beloved Central and ourselves into His all-wise and loving hands. This is the Lord's doing; it is marvelous in our eyes."

Thus closed the first decade and a half of Central's history. It had taken up a cause after another church had failed. In the beginning it had no building and only a handful of members, but it did have faith and hope. Now it had a beautiful cathedral-like church building, a congregation that numbered in the thousands, and a promise for the future that knew no bounds. Its motto of "Service to others" had guided it through the beginning years to a commanding position among its fellow churches.

CHAPTER 8

A Struggle for Survival

"A beacon light to all the land."

With the death of Pastor Stub on June 11, 1944, one era ended for Central Lutheran and another began. It was he who worked diligently with the founders of Central to build a strong structure. Throughout his quarter of a century of leadership, the objective of "service" was always present. It had become the watchword of Central, to fulfill the Biblical injunction that all men should live as brothers.

The years that went by during his pastorate were not easy ones. The troubles inherent in the founding of a new church were compounded when the great depression of the 1930's cast its shadow over the land. Yet the congregation grew and the influence of Central was felt not only in its own immediate area, but throughout the entire city. The new cathedral-church in which services were first held on Christmas Day, 1927, and which was dedicated on Palm Sunday, 1928, seated slightly over 3,000 worshippers. The membership numbered 1,600 at the time.

With its impressive new structure, Central grew in prestige and membership. Before another two years went by, the membership total had passed the 2,000 mark. The new organ was a superb instrument which added greatly to the impressiveness of the church services. Eugene Skaaden had been the first organist and choir director, followed by J. Victor Bergquist. In 1929, George Hultgren became the choir director and Marion Hutchinson the organist. In 1937, Peter Tkach became the choir director. The various organizations grew and prospered with the church itself. By the year 1933, the Sunday School had over 700 pupils enrolled, taught by a staff of 58 instructors. Heading the school for fifteen years was L. M. Brings.

The financial problems of the church were made more acute by the heavy bonding of $675,000 necessary to build the new church and the hard times which came soon after the new structure was completed. The construction had been financed by bonds which were covered by pledges and promissory notes signed by members of Central. However, the members themselves became victims of the Depression and many of them were unable to meet their pledges. At one time the situation was so bad that whereas the interest on the bonded indebtedness was $30,000 for the year, the church's income was only $21,000. Obviously its interest obligations could not be met.

It should be borne in mind that this was not a condition that confronted Central alone. The late 1920's had been unusually prosperous years and almost all business concerns and organizations had expanded optimistically. When the crash came, everyone was hurt, including many churches that had, like Central, built new buildings in the hope and expectation of continued good times.

For many years Central was forced to limp along, its members working desperately to keep their church a going concern. Consideration was given to offering the property for sale and moving into smaller quarters. An appeal was made to the president of the Norwegian Lutheran Church, the synodical body with which Central was affiliated, for financial assistance or some other aid so the church could survive. But the request for help was rejected, and Central was compelled to continue alone in solving its financial crisis. With the assistance and encouragement of Federal Judge Gunnar Nordbye in 1940, a plan of organization was worked out in federal court which provided for the eventual payment of all of the church bonds over a period of thirty and more years, but without interest. The bondholders were polled by the Court and consented to forego payment of interest and accept annual payments of principal over a period of thirty years. It was only through the untiring efforts of several of its members that the congregation was held together at this time.

"Then a miracle happened," stated a member of the church who had gone through those trying times at Central. "One of our men took it upon himself to save the church if he could possibly do so. He devoted almost his full time to the effort, and he succeeded. His plan was simple.

"He contacted all the bondholders by mail, almost a thousand of them, and offered to buy their church securities at a discount."

"In 1942, the Central Lutheran Church Endowment Fund had been started at the suggestion of this same member when a bequest of $1,000 was given to the church in the will of Mr. N. L. Enger. Here was a depository for the bonds that were now being purchased.

"After this member had purchased a bond at a discount, he would contact an individual and propose that he buy it and donate it to the Endowment Fund. Under the federal bankruptcy proceedings, the Northwestern National Bank was designated by the court to distribute the annual payments to all bondholders. Of course, the church was obligated to see that the annual payoffs were on deposit at the bank when due. Thus, it meant that the congregation itself would continue to pay off over the years every dollar of the original principal of $675,000. This eventually was done.

"When he finished his one-man campaign of buying bonds during a period of seven years, he had saved Central from financial collapse. In many instances, individuals paid for the bonds in full and donated them to the church. The crisis was over insofar as the bonded indebtedness was concerned. True, there were austere years ahead, but now there was little question about the solvency of the church."

Who was the man who "saved Central"? He has been a member of Central for fifty-five years, is still a member, still an active participant in the affairs of the church. However, he will not permit his name to be mentioned. In truth, at the time of his active labor on behalf of the church, there were few others who knew what was being done. The church officers and the Board of Trustees were not consulted. The purchase of bonds in this manner had no official sanction, even though Central congregation was still obligated to pay off every dollar of the original obligation under the court order. When interviewed, he said simply, "I did not do it for personal publicity or gratification. It was done for the benefit of the church."

This is the spirit that has guided the affairs of Central since its organization sixty years ago. This is why it has become known as the "Miracle Church."

Other auxiliary organizations, such as the Women's Guild, were especially active during these hard years. They raised thousands of dollars that went into the church treasury through gifts and dues in addition to that which was raised through projects such as dinners and entertainments.

During the first fifteen years, up to 1934, this hardworking organization had a gross income of $114,539.12. This stupendous sum was raised by direct gifts and dues, through entertainments and bazaars, through the serving of meals for every organization of the church. It was the Guild's contribution to the support of the church.

No one can ever begin to estimate the time and effort necessary for the accumulation of such a breath-taking sum through the accumulation of small cash. And, only God can possibly measure the grace and cheerfulness with which this service has been given. The contacts made through the ministrations of the Guild have been a splendid help in the growth of Central's membership during the first fifteen years of its existence. Hundreds had come to Central for the first time perhaps to enjoy what the members of the Guild had to offer, and were so impressed by the spirit of fellowship that their names sooner or later had come to appear on the church membership roster.

It was this spirit of service so early inculcated that determined the continuing unselfish activities of the women of Central up to the present time.

With the beginning of the war years, the hard times faded. The nation was in the midst of a life-and-death struggle for survival. Supplies and equipment of all kinds were desperately needed. Once more the wheels of industry began to turn. Jobs were now plentiful and the problems that had plagued Central for so long began to ease.

Pastor Stub's health began to fail and it was soon realized that his days as an active pastor were numbered. Wisely, he and the church officers counseled together. The work at Central was heavy and demanding. They would need a man who had the physical stamina and the spiritual strength to carry on that which had been begun so well. When Dr. Stub was a pastor in Stoughton, Wisconsin, he had in his congregation a youth named Elmer Hjortland who he had baptized and confirmed. A serious, capable lad, he had later entered the ministry, and had been ordained and married by Dr. Stub. After successful pastorates in Eau Claire and Milwaukee, Wisconsin, he was now serving as a chaplain in the United States Army.

Long hours of reflection and prayers preceded Pastor Stub's conclusion that Dr. Hjortland was his choice to succeed him as pastor of Central Luthern Church. The church officers and congregation agreed, for they had become well acquainted with him on his several visits to Central.

The decision to select Dr. Hjortland as his successor as senior pastor by Central was very pleasing to Dr. Stub. "Now," he said, "I can conclude my pastorate at Central Lutheran in peace and confidence. I know that Elmer will maintain the manpower of our congregation to carry on our service to others."

Dr. Hjortland, who was Dr. Stub's choice to be his successor as senior pastor, commented about his early impressions of Central Luthern Church:

"When Central's sanctuary was under construction, Dr. Stub enthusiastically told me his dream of a city church. I recall, as though it were only yesterday, the two of us walking around on the unfinished floor of the church-to-be, before the beginning of any superstructure. Dr. Stub pointed out to me where the chancel, the altar, the pulpit, and the two side chapels were to be located. I remember him saying that the pulpit must be out among the people — surrounded by the people rather than isolated or aloof from the congregation.

"This location of the pulpit was more than symbolism! It meant — to Dr. Stub and to the congregation — that the Word of God was to be in the midst of the people — in the center of the life and activity of the city of Minneapolis. This dream has been a visible, impressive reality from the beginning. Central Lutheran has provided guidance, inspiration, hope, and friendship to thousands of people in the Middle West. It has been a 'beacon light to all the land.'

"Countless numbers have come to the church with their personal troubles and found a listening ear and a strong, helping hand. Because of the size of Central, it is possible for a worshipper to attend as inconspicuously as Zacheus concealed himself among the leaves of the sycamore tree. To Central over the years have come the lonely, troubled, confused, bitter, and cynical as well as the devout worshippers who come to give praise and thanks to God. And, often to their surprise, the lonely, troubled, confused, bitter, and cynical found the Gospel and discovered that the Good News was also meant for them."

It was a heartening message that was brought to the congregation by the president, A. R. Hustad, at a special meeting following the regular Sunday morning services on November 21, 1943. He told of the work of the calling committee during the preceding year. After deliberate and conscientious exploration of the entire field, the committee had arrived at the unanimous decision to extend a call to the Rev. Elmer S. Hjortland. The congregation confirmed the recommendation of the committee.

It was almost two years before Dr. Hjortland could secure his release from the Army. He accepted the call when it was extended to him, praying the Central congregation to have patience in waiting for his release. God's work must be carried on in the army as well as back home, he reminded them. Meanwhile, he made several trips from his station in Camp Patrick Henry in Virginia to Minneapolis, making his presence felt at Central long before he assumed the pastorate. The Rev. Luther Roseland filled the pulpit and carried on the regular duties of the pastor during the interim.

When he met with the officers of the church after his acceptance of the call as senior pastor, he declared: "I'll take care of the spiritual needs of the congregation; you laymen are to provide for the financial and physical needs of the church. You get the money to support our program. Never expect me to ask a member for money, or to make a plea for funds from the pulpit. I don't want any conflict to exist between me and the members because of money."

Then he went on to declare: "I am going to be concerned about all people who are not members of any church, and I will devote my major efforts to bring them into our membership."

In this way he determined his program — to serve others. Because of the strategic location of Central, Dr. Stub had discovered that 75% of all pastoral acts were with nonmembers during his twenty-five years of service. This program of service to others was to be continued during the future years — even up to 1980.

Sunday, August 19, 1945, was a significant day in the history of Central Lutheran. On that day the Rev. Hjortland was installed as senior pastor and a new era began for the church.

The laymen of Central were hungry for leadership. There had been no forward-moving activity during the decline of Dr. Stub's health, resulting, finally, in his death. Their energies were waiting to be harnessed for action after two years of comparative inactivity while waiting for Pastor Hjortland to arrive. But this was an auspicious opportunity for the new pastor and he plunged immediately into marshaling the forces of laymen to make a renewed start. The time was ripe for new programs and new incentives.

Every area of church activity was overhauled and new impetus was given to the overall program of the church. But all changes and innovations were made to promote the ideal of serving the community. The motto of "The Servant Church" was not forgotten.

Meeting with all organizations of the church, Dr. Hjortland proposed revamping programs and organizations. Special emphasis was given to highlighting the music of the church. "The Cathedral Hour" and "Christmas at Central" were a result. Additional choirs were organized to include children as well as adults. "The Ushers' Society" was reorganized with new methods of procedure. The Evening Guild was organized in May 1945. In 1946, the Young Married Couples' Club was started, followed by the organization of the Junior Guild. Later the Senior Couples' Club began. The Sun Dial Club was started soon to serve retired persons 65 years of age and over who lived in the vicinity of Central, the majority not members of Central. They still continue to meet twice a week, with their own officers, and a scheduled program of activities. Special attention was given to the youth activities of the church, beginning with the Central Hi Night in September 1948. In 1948, a Mothers' Club was started that sponsored the nursery, which is still in operation. We have just enumerated a few of the 115 organizations of the church that had their inception after Dr. Hjortland's arrival.

To assist Pastor Hjortland and his assistants to keep in touch with the ever-increasing membership, a pastor's cabinet was created in 1946. The area served by the church was divided into districts, 18 in all, and chairmen and leaders were assigned to each district. Mrs. Norman Nelson served as director of the cabinet for several years. This was a method to keep lines of communication open between the pastoral staff and members.

During 1947, plans were made to conduct a finance campaign, having for its purpose the reduction of the church debt and the creation of a fund to construct a building that would provide additional Sunday School space. A building fund campaign was conducted in February of that year by Fred Shearer of the H. P. Demand Co. of Chicago with a goal to raise $200,000. The goal was reached!

Dr. Hjortland was a dynamic and popular preacher. The Sunday morning services and the midweek Lenten meetings drew capacity crowds. Each Sunday the service continued to be broadcast over the St. Olaf College radio station WCAL, reaching thousands of individuals over a wide area of the Northwest who were unable to attend in person. So whenever they came to Minneapolis, many of them decided to visit the great cathedral they had heard about, attend the Sunday services, and actually see the preachers they had listened to over the air.

When Pastor Hjortland announced that he would be at his office every Thursday night from seven to midnight to visit, listen, and counsel anyone who was looking for understanding help, a steady procession of people came to the pastor's study. He has written recently about his counseling service at Central: "All were represented — jilted maidens and men, emotionally disturbed children, frustrated and bitter wives, husbands burdened beyond their resources, alcoholics, young people lost in the big city and trapped in vices to which they had become slaves, theologically disturbed students, parents and children at odds with one another, suicide-prone people, men and women with records of crime — and occasionally a few to say 'thank you' for the Sunday morning services.

"Every conceivable sin was confessed. Sometimes the guilt was imaginery, then again it was deep and took much prayer and fasting (discipline) to expose the trouble and find assurance of a way to daylight. Often people who came for counsel left with a new understanding of the grace of God and a way opened to them which enabled them to find inner peace and meaning to life. Both young and old discovered the church, Central Lutheran, was a 'friend.'

"How wise was the counsel and how permanent the change, only God knows, but the people who were 'seeking' knew the church was there to help. Many became members of a church near their home. No effort was made to get them to join Central or change whatever religious affiliation may have existed.

"The outreach of Central was due primarily to a clear concept of the gospel of Christ presented in the language of disciplined love. The pulpit was never used as a political platform or a theological rostrum. Those who have come to Central over the years have been inspired by the music of able musicians and great choirs dedicated to the glory of God. As one worshipper expressed it: 'The services at Central send me through the week with music in my heart.'"

During 1947, the young people of the church embarked upon a notable project of their own, the raising of funds to send their Youth Pastor, the Rev. Maynard Iverson, to the World Conference of Christian Youth in Oslo, Norway. It was also during this full year in the life of the church that the Rev. J. O. Holum joined the staff as minister in charge of visitation.

The Senior Choir, under the direction of Peter Tkach, had grown in numbers until now it had a membership of over a hundred. It was one of the best-known choirs of the city, famous for its annual production of the "Messiah" at Christmastime. This was undertaken with the aid of the choir of St. Mark's Episcopal Cathedral. The Central group also became famous for its "Cathedral Hour," given at the beginning of the Lenten season. Frequently the choir went "on the air," especially in observance of the various religious days.

The Memorial Fund, created at the time of Dr. Stub's death, prospered. Sponsored by the Men's Club of Central, it received hundreds of contributions ranging from $5 to $200. The objective was $10,000, which was reached shortly. In November, L. M. Brings, chairman of the Board of Trustees, announced, "It is the hope of the Board that there will be an increase in this fund which will be dedicated to parish work in the downtown district."

The Rev. Orvis Hanson served Central as a youth pastor, but left in 1945 to accept a call to a mission field in China. On the Pacific Coast, awaiting sailing instructions, he was notified that the Mission Board had changed its plans on operations in the Orient for the time being. When news of this happening reached Central's calling committee, it immediately met in special session and extended an invitation to the Rev. Hanson to return to Central. Shortly after the first of the year, the Rev. Hanson again resumed his duties as Youth Pastor at Central. That same year, the Rev. Maynard Iverson was installed as another of Central's youth pastors, indicative of the high value that the church placed on the religious life of their young people. The Rev. R. C. Reinholtzen was the assistant pastor at Central at this time.

Early in the history of Central Church the newspaper called "The Spirit of Central" began publication. It has persisted down to the present time. Its pages are filled with newsworthy items of interest and concern at the time of release. Issued once a month, it features items not carried in the regular weekly bulletin.

During Dr. Hjortland's ministry at Central, he strove to make *The Spirit of Central* a personal means of communication between himself and his staff and the congregation.

"When I read this paper each month, I felt that each item is directed to me personally," commented a long-time member of Central. "This was especially true of Dr. Hjortland's own column which was called *The Pastor's Study*. He had a way of writing which directed his thoughts to each reader. I got into the habit of glancing first at the front-page headlines, then turning to the Pastor's column on page two, when the paper came into my hands. It was like a sport's fan taking a quick look at the front page of a newspaper, then turning to the sports' section, his main interest."

A short item in the December 1947 issue of the Central *Spirit* illustrates the point made by this appreciative member. Pastor Hjortland wrote: "I hope that during the customary rush and hurry of this Christmas season we will remember above all that we are Christians. Not only should we be pleasant, cheerful and helpful, not only should we sing carols and exchange gifts, but we should give to those who need help but cannot return the kindness. We should gather in our churches and give thanks to Him who is the Creator and Giver of all good things. To all the members and friends of Central Lutheran Church, I earnestly wish a memorable Christmas — one of peace in your hearts, sunshine on your countenance, and love in your home."

In his column in another issue, he wrote: "We have a number of tithers in our church. None feels it a burden. Compare what you spend for pleasure, for luxuries, for cosmetics and tobacco with what you give to the Lord's work. Can you really ask God's blessing on your use of all of your earthly goods? On the day of reckoning will he say to you, 'You are a faithful and wise steward'?"

Surviving Incorporators and Charter Members, Palm Sunday, 1949

Church Planning Conference, 1959, northern Minnesota camp

President Don Carson turns the first spade of ground for the
Sunday School building.

Senior Choir, Holy Week, 1949

Laying the Cornerstone, Sunday School Building

Members gather for the dedication of the Sunday School building.

The completed Sunday School building

Beginning the construction of the Parish House.

Cornerstone laying of the Parish House

Dedication of the Parish House, August 4, 1957

Mrs. Moody and Mrs. Prestholdt, two of the original founders,
looking at the Founders Plaque.

The daughter of Dr. Stub, Mrs. Ann Lunden, and grandson Larry,
examine the Founders Plaque.

Minneapolis Recognition Banquet for Dr. Gornitzka

Following the Easter season that year, Dr. Hjortland wrote with great rejoicing: "A glorious season of fellowship with God reached its climax on Easter morning. During Holy Week over 3,000 persons received Holy Communion. On 'Easter Sunday a conservative estimate was 10,000 in attendance ... You will enjoy and benefit by your membership in Central to the degree to which you truly give yourself to the church."

Although the tone of the column was understandably serious, there were occasions on which he resorted to humor, usually to underscore a human frailty that could be looked upon with a degree of compassion. One of such items was labeled *A Fable*. It read: "At eight o'clock last evening I said to my wife, 'Let's go out for a spin.' In ten minutes she was ready and we set out. We started to cross the river, but our car ran off the open bridge and quickly sank beneath the water. Fortunately a big dog on the bank saw the accident and jumped into the river and saved us. Then it ran up to the highway and barked for help. You smile: What do you find incredible about this? I see . . . the part about my wife being ready in ten minutes . . ."

One can well understand the favor which this column found with its readers.

In addition, *The Spirit of Central* contained many other articles of interest to Central's members. Coming events were headlines: "St. Olaf Day at Central, May 2nd"; "Central Kneels at Bethlehem's Cradle." Organizational work was given: The Choir, the Evening Guild, Couple's Club, Women's Guild, Men's Club, Martha Mission, a full page called the *Youth's Corner*. There was something for everybody, young and old, men and women, members and nonmembers. It was an all-inclusive church paper presenting Central Lutheran as it was month by month. It began this presentation in the 1920's; it continues throughout the 1980's.

A forward step was taken at Central Lutheran when Leif R. Larson, for 25 years a YMCA secretary, became the church's first business manager. Charles Thiele had served as office manager during 1920-1925. Leif Larson's appointment was the first of its kind in the Evangelical Lutheran Synod and one of the first in the nation. His duties were to take care of all matters relating to business administration and financing of the church as well as assisting the various organizations and program projects. Mr. Larson took office on January 1, 1950.

Central's Sunday Bulletin for September 19, 1920, carried this item: "Beginning next Thursday at 8 p.m., the pastor will conduct a 'Bible Hour' in the Sunday School auditorium. This is a new venture with us. Come and help us make this a blessed and profitable hour. Remember also this hour in your prayers."

In another issue was printed this item: "The Mid-week Bible Hour has read the Book of Exodus and is continuing with portions of the Book of Numbers to round out the picture of the life of Moses, the great leader of Israel. A cordial welcome is extended to all to attend our meetings." The date of this issue was 1950, thirty years later.

Such has been the spirit of Central, that has made this church great.

CHAPTER 9

The "Greater Central" Concept Is Born

"If God be with us, who can be against us?"
—Romans 8:31

Following the war years, Central continued its steady growth. The nation was booming economically, a condition that was reflected in the affairs of the church. A great shortage of everyday household goods and appliances had developed during the war when the country's economy had been geared to the production of war materials. A conversion to civilian production proved to be a quick and easy transition, and soon the factories were humming with the making of products designed not to kill, but to produce a better way of life. Many predicted that the new era would be of short duration, but as time passed it became increasingly evident that this would not be the case. With better times came more money in the pockets of wage-earners, some of which inevitably found its way into Central's treasury.

Attendance increased at services, for Dr. Hjortland's preaching was very effective. So large were the crowds that came to hear him that a second Sunday morning service was begun. Peter Tkach's health declined and the Rev. Johan Thorson was named as Minister of Music to take his place. At this time, the Rev. Warren Sigwalt became a member of the church staff as youth pastor.

The first concept of a "Greater Central" was conceived by the chairman of the Board of Trustees in 1948 when he proposed that the church purchase the two houses on Fourth Avenue South next to the old church as the start of a land acquisition program to provide space for future building expansion and parking facilities. There was a difference of opinion among the members of the board and it was decided to call a special meeting of the congregation to accept or reject the proposal. A motion was passed unanimously to proceed with the purchase. Thus began an extensive program of land acquisition that has continued to this day. Farsighted thinking has resulted in adequate parking areas for members attending the church services.

Because of the expanding enrollment of the Sunday School, it was decided that larger quarters were urgently needed to adequately continue on the program outlined. The land needed for a building was now owned by the church. A committee was appointed which decided to conduct a special Every Member Canvass in November 1950, under the direction of Leif Larson. More than five hundred volunteers were organized to call on every family in the congregation. Pledges of $138,480 were secured, which included $75,000 for the Sunday School building fund. Following this canvass, a second drive was conducted to bring new members into Central's folds. It resulted in securing 445 additional men and women to add to Central's membership.

When the double services were inaugurated on October 2, 1949, it was decided that they should be identical in nature. The senior pastor, the Rev. Hjortland, preached at both sessions, assisted by the Rev. J. O. Holum. The plan worked well, the total attendance exceeding that of the single service previously conducted. The first service was held at 9:30 a.m., and the second at eleven o'clock. The Chapel Choir, assisted by some of the members of the Senior Choir, provided the music for the early service.

The inflationary tendency resulting from the expanding economy, was reflected in the cost of a lutefisk dinner which was served at the church by the Women's Guild on the evening of October 28, 1949. During the depth of the depression, such dinner cost per person was 35 cents. Later the price was increased to 50 cents. Tickets for the 1949 dinner sold for $1.25, a price that would have been considered prohibitive only a few years before.

At this time there were five pastors who carried on the spiritual work at Central: Senior Pastor Hjortland; his assistant, the Rev. Holum, who also had charge of the Thursday evening Bible hours; the youth pastors, the Rev. Sigwalt and the Rev. Bergh; and the minister of music, the Rev. Thorson.

An example of the outreach of Central was manifested by the assistance given to a group of displaced persons who had just arrived in Minneapolis from Latvia. There were a sufficient number to justify organizing a congregation, which they did, with the Rev. Peter Langins as their pastor. They were invited to use Old Central to conduct their worship services and activities without any cost to them. They started in October 1949 and continued until they moved into their own church in 1954.

Information that was considered vital to an understanding of the full significance of the church was disseminated well among the members of the congregation. The workers of the church asked in a communication to the general membership as the 1949 ended and a new year began:

DO YOU KNOW

. . . THAT in 1949 there were 112 groups organized and functioning in Central Lutheran Church?

. . . THAT the aggregate attendance of these groups last year was 77,119, or an average of 23 persons per meeting?

. . . THAT in the past two years, $151,000 has been paid on the funded debt, leaving a balance of $252,251?

. . . THAT the operating budget for 1949 was $147,920 and that of this amount, $45,567 was for debt retirement and $22,880 was for missions?

. . . THAT the Every Member Canvass is merely a convenient way of encouraging regular weekly contributions to further the work of this church?

. . . THAT you will be much happier in 1950 if you give regularly for the extension of His work?

Ground was broken for the new Sunday School building and the first section of a parish house, and the intensive campaign staged by the church officials had as one of its primary objectives the furtherance of this project.

The November 1950 issue of *The Spirit of Central* contained a fable that brought the point home to its readers. It was entitled:

Tipping and Tithing

Now it came to pass on a Day at noon that the Editor was Guest of a certain Rich man. And the Lunch was enjoyed at a popular Restaurant. And the Waiters were very efficient. And the food was good.

Now when the End of the Meal was at Hand, the Waiter brought unto the Host the Check. And the Host examined it, frowned a bit, but made no Comment.

But as we arose to depart, I observed that he laid some Coins under the Edge of the Plate. However, I knew what the Denomination of the Coins was.

But the Waiter, who stood nearby, smiled happily, which being interpreted means that the Tip was satisfactory.

Now, with such customs we are all familiar. And this Parable entereth not into the Merits or Demerits of Tipping.

But as I meditated on the Coins that become Tips throughout our Nation, I began to think of Tips and Tithes. For the proverbial Tip should be at least a Tithe, lest the Waiter or the Waitress turn against you.

And as I continued to think on these Things, it came unto me that few people come to treat their God as well as they honor their Waiter. For they give unto the Waiter a Tithe, but unto God they give Whatsoever they think will get them by.

Verily, doth Man fear the Waiter more than he feareth God? And doth he love God less than he loveth the Waiter?

Truly, truly, a Man and his Money are beyond Understanding!

Countless men who would not think of leaving a tip of less than ten percent thought of this parable when the time came to fill out their annual pledge cards. Many of them had never thought of the implications involved in tipping — afraid to leave less than ten percent for their waiter, but grudgingly giving but one or two percent to their God.

The pastor, his wife, and the church officers were ever on the alert for means of promoting the goals of Central and to bring into closer union the members of the church. In this effort, the various organizations played an important part. It was in the autumn of the year 1951 that Dr. and Mrs. Hjortland began the practice of inviting the members of the congregation to the parsonage for the purpose of becoming better acquainted, they with the pastor and his wife; the minister and his wife with them. The congregation was large and it was difficult for the pastor to become well enough acquainted with all of them to even recognize them when they met. To call them by name or to know their problems was impossible.

Dr. Hjortland commented, "Often I would pass someone on the street who would say, 'I am a member of your congregation; my name is . . .' and in this way we would meet and become acquainted. This always pleased me, for I have thousands in my congregation to meet and to get to know. They have but one senior pastor."

Inviting members to the parsonage was not only a gesture of friendship and good will, but was also a practical way of furthering the work of the church and thereby better achieving the objectives of Central. This practice was continued throughout the remainder of Pastor Hjortland's term of service at Central.

More than thirty years had now gone by since Central Lutheran Church began its work in downtown Minneapolis. It had carried out its ambitious program of service to the community faithfully. Nevertheless, it had not neglected the broader aspects of its program, carrying its good works even into foreign lands through its contributions to the missionary endeavors. Now it decided to make its aid of a more personal nature by supporting its own missionary abroad. The Rev. Conrad M. Aamodt was sent by Central to far-off Japan where he spread the Christian message among the people of that land. During the second World War, Japan had been one of America's enemies, but in its defeat it showed a spirit of contrition and a desire to Westernize its country. In this worthy purpose, Central had a desire to participate.

Following the successful completion of its Every-Member campaign at this time, the trustees of the church decided to proceed with the first phase of their building program. One half of the anticipated cost of this first phase had been paid into the building fund. A Sunday School unit was badly needed, for the present quarters were overcrowded and the work of the department was being hampered by the inadequate facilities. In keeping with the avowed intent of the church to establish a lasting tradition, the shovel that had been used in the ground-breaking ceremony in 1926, when construction of the new church was begun, was now again brought forth.

On the last day of the year but one, the frozen ground was broken and the new endeavor was blessed. Everyone knew that the road ahead would be a rugged one, for expanding the facilities of a church is never an easy project to undertake. However, the work progressed and on March 25, 1952, the cornerstone of the building was laid. On October 26 it was dedicated. The cost was a quarter of a million dollars, but by January 1, 1953, this amount had been accumulated and the building was debt free.

It was on a cold Sunday morning that the ground-breaking ceremony took place. Snow covered the frozen soil. Don Carson, president of the congregation, turned the first bit of ground, beginning a project that would continue on until a new and beautiful structure had been completed. Hundreds of members of the congregation, and others as well, gathered about. In the forefront were the children, their faces reflecting the happiness of the moment. It was for them that this was taking place.

Optimism was the order of the day. The next day L. M. Brings, chairman of the Board of Trustees, wrote to the Rev. Hjortland:

"As the year 1951 comes to a close, we feel impelled to write you a letter of thanks and appreciation for your leadership and service to Central Lutheran during the year.

"The congregation last January authorized the Board of Trustees to proceed with building plans for the first unit of the Parish House. Yesterday our President broke the ground that started us on the construction of the Sunday School building. It has been a great year of progress, for which we all are grateful."

It had, indeed, been a year of progress. Central was truly moving forward in its great work.

With the dedication of the new building, the church congregation and its officials were able to say with feeling in the October issue of *The Spirit of Central* — a publication in which they exultantly called their church *The Greater Central* — "All through the year, Greater Central provides a spiritual home for thousands of people. It is a center for religious instruction of youth and a place for all to receive Christian guidance. It is a sanctuary for hearts that are heavy laden. It is a place for people to come when they need the things of the spirit. We are in a unique position. Our church stands at the crossroads of a great metropolitan city. It ministers to people of all walks of life. It has a large home mission program. It sets the standards in many phases of church life. As we look ahead to 1953, our stewardship is clear. We must meet the challenge of a Greater Central in order that more people can be won for Christ. Our needs are heavy. Look forward to 1953, eager to do your part."

Central was truly a church that ministered to all. It had a great responsibility and its obligations were heavy. Its ability to measure up to its responsibilities and to meet its obligations were limited only by the willingness of its members to support it with their money, their assistance, and their prayers. The full pages of pictures carried in the autumn issue of Central's paper told a graphic story of the church's history, the many personalities involved, giving an indication of one of the reasons why the "Miracle Church" had succeeded so well in the goals that had been set for it at its founding.

America was again at war, this time in faraway Korea. As the year ended, the holiday season at Central was marred by the unhappiness of the many sons and brothers of members who were so far from home, fighting in a strange and cold land. To the fifty-six men of Central who were stationed in our own camps, boxes of candy were sent as a token of appreciation from the congregation. Abroad were forty-two others, and to each of them was sent a box of food. The replies that came back to the senders were heartwarming.

"It is wonderful to know that the folks back home have not forgotten us," said one lad, stationed abroad, whose thoughts at the Christmas season were of his family and friends at home.

Another group of young people was similarly recognized. It was the college students who were attending school outside of their home area. A list of these members of Central was published in order to let others know where they could be reached. This was but another of the ways in which Central continued to serve, even though those concerned were away from their home community and the church with which they were affiliated. Baptism, weddings and deaths were similarly reported regularly in the church paper.

When one hundred and fifty-two members were admitted to Central shortly after the new year began, the membership list exceeded five thousand. Several thousand others regarded Central Lutheran as their home church although they had not officially affiliated with it. Membership was always encouraged by the pastor and other officials, but it was of secondary importance. "Service to all" was the goal of Central regardless of the status of those served.

It was during the year 1953 that Marion Hutchinson observed her 25th anniversary as organist at Central. It was in September of 1928 that she had succeeded J. Victor Bergquist. Her work was not only that which the congregation was made aware of during divine services on Sunday. She had long ago given organ recitals over radio station WCAL at St. Olaf College in Northfield each Sunday afternoon. In the church itself she gave a vesper service on Sunday afternoon, one each month, featuring Bach selections. On Wednesday evenings she met regularly with the Chapel Choir and the next evening was given to the Senior Choir. Regularly on Saturdays she was at Central's organ, practicing the numbers that were to be played the next day for the enjoyment of so many listeners. From time to time special concerts were given, making the name of Central Lutheran familiar to untold thousands of radio listeners. During her long stay at Central she was honored by being given a fellowship in the American Guild of Organists. This was the highest earned degree available for organists, obtained only after undergoing an exhaustive examination.

Paying tribute to Miss Hutchinson during her anniversary year, Pastor Hjortland said, "Central Lutheran Church is known far and wide for a variety of reasons. One oft-mentioned reason is the wonderful organ music of Marion Hutchinson. The skillful manner in which this instrument is played by her has added immeasurably to the renown of this church."

On August 29, 1954, Frederic Hilary became minister of music at Central — a full-time position — and Joyce Hilary as the organist. Again a forward-moving stride was made in strengthening the music program of the church.

At this time there were five vocal groups at Central, with a membership of over two hundred and fifty. They were the Cherub Choir, made up of children of grades one through three; the Carol Choir, of older children; the Chapel Choir, the Senior Choir, and the Central Chorale.

The practice of holding open house at the parsonage continued with gratifying results. A note in the church paper's column entitled *Pastor's Study*, December 1954, gives an interesting view of this feature of the church's work. Pastor Hjortland wrote: "We had 'Open House' at the parsonage on Sunday afternoon, November 14. We anticipated that if the weather were bad we would have about 300 visitors, and if pleasant, about 500. Our estimate was off by a considerable number. Well over a thousand people visited the parsonage that day. Since this was the first Open House to be held since the new parsonage was built, we were interested in the comments made about it. It is obvious that our members are pleased with it as planned and built by the board of trustees. Already quite a few organizations have met in the parsonage and it will be put to good use for many years to come."

The year 1955 marked the tenth year of devoted service given by Pastor Hjortland to Central Lutheran Church. The decade had shown consistently the character of the senior pastor's tenure. The work so worthily performed by Central's first minister, Dr. Stub, had been carried on and enriched by his successor. In many ways the members of Central had expressed their deep feelings toward him. The same year that was to end his ten years of service was also to bring to a finish his pastorate at Central.

When the annual meeting of the congregation was held on January 25, a sincere resolution was adopted unanimously by the members. Its words told of the great regard that they held for the Rev. Hjortland. It read:

Whereas Pastor Elmer S. Hjortland during 1955 will have completed ten years of devoted service to Central Lutheran Church; and

Whereas he has performed all his duties as senior pastor of Central Lutheran Church with diligence, keen insight and understanding, and has successfully united the membership to work together in the furtherance of the work of the church; and

Whereas we have witnessed great spiritual and material growth in the advancement of the Christian cause in our congregation; and

Whereas he has expanded the influence of Central Lutheran Church by his appearance as a speaker before many groups in the community and the nation and has participated in many civic activities for the betterment of society; and

Whereas he has utilized his experience in the Christian ministry to help hundreds of individuals to face and solve their personal problems by expert counseling and guidance; and

Whereas he has opened up new vistas of thinking by our members in the accomplishment of a Greater Central; therefore

Be it resolved that the congregation of Central Lutheran Church in annual meeting assembled do hereby express its gratitude to Almighty God for His guidance of our senior pastor in all his manifold accomplishments during the past ten years, and that by a rising vote we individually and collectively express our appreciation and pledge our support and cooperation to him in the remaining years of his ministry in Central Lutheran Church.

The resolution was a worthy one, well deserved. It was ironic that the hope was implied in it that his additional years at Central should be many. Before the year ended, Dr. Hjortland resigned his position at Central to accept a call to Oak Park, Illinois, a suburb of Chicago. His final service at Central was conducted on October 9, 1955, following his return from a world tour. He had, as the church's senior pastor, won his way into the hearts of the thousands of persons in the Midwest, members and nonmembers of his congregation. His record was one of glorious achievement. Well could the congregation look back upon the resolution which they had passed earlier in the year, to view it almost as an ominous portent. The praise which they had given him in unstinted measure had gone far beyond the confines of the local community. Others, too, had heard and heeded.

The following statement recently sent the author by Dr. Hjortland might have been written upon his departure for Oak Park, Illinois.

"There is a very significant reason why Central Lutheran has been a church of the people. Laymen have not only listened and prayed, but have been 'doers of the Word and not hearers only.' There are some laymen who take an interest for a short period and then fade out of sight. They quickly 'weary of well doing.' Central, on the other hand, has been blessed with men and women who year after year gave time, money, and energy to the work of the church. They gave a contagious enthusiasm to the service they rendered. They rose above personal feelings or hurt pride and put the church first. There are very few churches in the country with a history of intelligent lay leadership equal to Central Lutheran. The city of Minneapolis keeps growing in size, and her problems — social, economic, moral — are those of all large cities, but the church has 'maintained her spiritual glow.' This sustained spiritual power comes, in a large measure, from the members of the church who are responsible Christians.

"Central Lutheran has been blessed with laymen who were not just names on the church records, but living, vital Christians who felt the 'divine restlessness' until they assumed a share of the responsibility for the total mission of the church. Not only men, but women in equal number have prayed, served, led, and 'spoken up' when words counted. Here, also, numerous names come to mind, but again a name comes to the forefront — Mrs. Serine Prestholdt. This gentle, good woman with a fine mind and warm heart could always be counted on to be loyal and cheerful. She was no quitter and never allowed the irritations of the moment or the slowness of others to dim her spirits or slacken her service to the Lord. Such people are the salt of the earth.

"May Central Lutheran always be blessed by a pulpit surrounded by the congregation and worshippers who become moral and spiritual leaven in the community."

As is characteristic of Elmer Hjortland he had accepted a call to United Lutheran Church in Oak Park, Illinois, because he decided that the congregation needed his services to give a renewed spiritual emphasis to its program. He did accomplish his objective after serving several years as the senior pastor.

Then another call for help was sent to him by the Westchester Lutheran Church in Los Angeles and he became the senior pastor. The congregation had a few internal problems, but with the cooperation of faithful members, these problems were solved and the congregation became an unusual energetic, spiritual force in the community. Dr. Hjortland wrote: "I accepted the call to Westchester with the understanding that after reaching 70 I would resign and assume a lesser role."

However, he accepted a call to Our Saviour's Lutheran Church in downtown Los Angeles as assistant to Rev. Myrus Knutson who began his ministry with him in Milwaukee as an assistant. After a year and a half, he became the interim pastor at Newport Harbor Lutheran Church during the terminal illness of their pastor.

After serving two years as Vice President of Golden Valley Lutheran College, he accepted a call to Sun City, Arizona, where with a small group a congregation was organized and eventually property was purchased and adequate worship facilities were constructed. Visitors have praised the church edifice as not only worshipful but one of the most beautiful houses of worship in Arizona. Within a few years the membership grew rapidly to approximately 1200 persons.

Recently he stepped down from the position of senior pastor and new serves as the visitation pastor.

Dr. Hjortland writes: "Mildred has had several operations for eye problems. Since 1975 she has been totally blind. Though this has severely handicapped her, she has accepted with good grace and patience her limitations. We enjoy Sun City and the people very much. It is a different type of ministry. The people are mature. Many of them have been faithful church members in other congregations and communities, while others who neglected their church responsibilities have come to a clear understanding of what the Gospel means for them. When the mask is removed the person behind the mask is always much more delightful and interesting to know. What the future holds for us, we do not know, but we do know the Lord runs the show and it is for us to fit into His plans."

Dr. Elmer S. Hjortland exemplifies all the qualities we expect to find in a true servant of our Lord. The members of Central Lutheran Church are grateful for his dedicated service to them as their pastor. He is truly a man of God.

For this third time in thirty-five years, Central was faced with the need of securing a new pastor to lead them into the uncertain future. The task ahead was not an easy one.

CHAPTER **10**

Central's Influence Spreads Worldwide

"A Landmark Church of Our Faith"

During its long history, Central Lutheran Church has availed itself of the services of student assistants to the senior pastor. Young and forceful, they added the element of energetic enthusiasm to the experience of the pastor with whom they served. One of these students was A. Reuben Gornitzka, who had assisted Dr. Stub during 1942-1943. He was favorably and well remembered by many of Central's members. His pastorate in Milwaukee had been a highly successful one.

During his stay at Our Savior's Lutheran Church in Milwaukee, from 1944 to the time he was chosen to be Central's senior pastor, the membership of his church had increased from 600 to 4200. A million-dollar church had also been built, attesting to the faith of his members. He had been active in civic and community affairs in Milwaukee. He came from an able and respected family. His father, the Rev. O. Gornitzka, was a former dean and later a member of the faculty of the Lutheran Bible Institute in Minneapolis.

Such was the nature of the man to whom a call was now issued. During the interim, the Rev. J. O. Holum, visitation pastor at Central, was named to serve as acting minister.

Without interruption, the full work of the church went on. The Christmas season arrived with its many activities; the Every Member Canvass was made; the Sunday School presented its annual Yuletide program, the servicemen were faithfully remembered; the many organizations completed their end-of-year activities and made plans for the New Year of 1956.

Such was the organization of Central Lutheran that no one man dominated the church, and the members were completely indoctrinated in their responsibilities. True, the senior pastor was its head and upon him and his leadership abilities depended to a great extent the effectiveness of the church program. However, Central had more than 5,000 members. They constituted the church; the pastor was one of them, always in a position of guidance and leadership, but never the church itself. The laymen continued to assume the task of carrying on the service program of the church.

The installation of the Rev. Gornitzka as Central's third senior pastor took place in an impressive ceremony on February 12, 1956. At both of the Sunday morning services, the congregation witnessed the installation. Dr. F. A. Schiotz, president of the Evangelical Lutheran Church, speaking at the ceremony, declared, "I know of no Lutheran congregation in this great land of ours that enjoys the good will and the concern of Lutherans everywhere, irrespective of synodical affiliation, in the degree that Central Lutheran enjoys that privilege. In the lives of the people of the ELC, there is a deep affection and intercessory concern for Central Lutheran Church."

They were not mere words that he spoke to Central's assembled thousands that cold Sunday morning. For over a quarter of a century this church had spread its influence for good over the community. Its workers had gone far afield in obeying the Great Teacher's injunction to "love they neighbor as thyself." The fruits of their labors were many. Pastor Gornitzka was entering a fertile field where his abilities would be used to the advantage of many persons.

So numerous were the activities of Central that additional staff members were needed. A parish worker, Miss Jurine Fjore, began work in September; Harold McCullough, a student at Luther Seminary and a member of Central, was made a student assistant to the pastor; the Rev. Karl Brevik was installed as assistant pastor on June 24, 1956, synod convention Sunday. The Rev. L. F. Scheie became the Visitation Pastor on July 1, 1958, and the Rev. Orin D. Thompson joined the pastoral staff on April 1, 1961.

A Bible camp on Clearwater Lake west of Minneapolis attracted many of Central's young people during the summer, in cooperation with other ELC churches.

Progress was being made in the extension of the service program of the church. A Blood Donors' Club was organized by the Young Couples' Club in 1956. At the end of the year it served 625 individuals, which was increased to 946 by the end of 1958. In October 1963, the Bethel Bible Series of classes were started, which has grown to such large proportions that over half the congregation has completed the courses up to the present time. In June 1957, Mrs. Gertrude Frisch became the Food Services Director, assuming charge of planning the dinners and other social activities of the church. She continued in this position until 1967.

The Toastmasters' Club was started in January 1956, the first Lutheran church in the city to organize such a club. In 1959, the noonday Men's Luncheon Group was started.

To indicate the recognition of Central in the community, Dr. Gornitzka was appointed Chairman of the 1957 Fund Campaign of the Mayor's Commission on Human Relations. Later Dr. Gornitzka served on the Minneapolis Auditorium Committee involved in the building of an addition to the old auditorium as well as modernizing the old structure.

The *Lutheran Brotherhood Bond* for May 1956, featured Central in one of a series of articles entitled "Landmark Churches of Our Faith," calling attention of the other churches to the work being done by Central.

Ever since Central Lutheran Church was founded in 1919, "Old Central" had been utilized for various activities. It was the building which the "Courageous Twelve" had purchased, to become Central Lutheran. In it, services were held for the first eight years. Built in 1883, it was known as Central Baptist Church until its sale in 1919, It was a solid structure, but no longer serving adequately the needs of Central Lutheran.

An invitation had previously been extended to the Lutheran World Federation to hold its 1957 International Assembly in Minneapolis at Central Lutheran Church. This hastened the necessity to provide enlarged facilities to adequately take care of delegates for committee sessions.

Plans were now made to replace the old building with a new structure, carefully planned to fill the immediate and future needs of Central. Conforming to the architectural pattern of the church, it would be known as the second unit of the "Greater Central" program of parish house construction. In it were to be the offices of the church, classrooms for instructional purposes, music rehearsal rooms, lounges for both youths and adults, a multiple-purpose fellowship hall, a recreation hall for youth groups, and nursery facilities. The estimated cost at the time of planning was $700,000, a figure that was eventually exceeded due to the rising costs of labor and materials that occurred during the postwar years.

Also planned at this time was a third unit, a memorial chapel that would seat 250 persons, to be used for weddings, baptisms, funerals, daily worship services, meditations, and youth assemblies. It thoughtfully provided for additional facilities for a program that recognized small groups as an effective way of reaching young people and influencing them spiritually. This third unit has not yet been constructed, but is one of the projects to be undertaken later.

Work began on the second unit at once, and the old structure that had witnessed so many spiritual happenings during its three quarters of a century of existence was demolished in June 1956.

An activity initiated by the Rev. Gornitzka at this time became a regular feature of Central's service. A one-hour service to be held every Sunday evening was begun. Its goal, said the pastor, was "an informal, friendly, worshipful, inspiring hour." Held in the main sanctuary, the service included a twilight hymn sing, a quiet prayer period, worshipful music, and a personal message by Pastor Gornitzka or one of the other ministers of the church.

"I ask of you," said the Rev. Gornitzka, "to visit this service at least once. It may be something for which you, too, have been looking."

At the first service, held on September 23, four hundred persons were present. Two weeks later, over six hundred attended. Following each evening service, coffee was served by the Senior League so that those attending would have an opportunity to become better acquainted.

When Pastor Orin Thompson joined the staff he was placed in charge of the Sunday evening program. He comments about his activity:

"The vespers continued as usual, but we began to have special programs from 9 to 10 p.m. the *year round*. (Coffee is served in the Fellowship Hall from 8:30 to 9 p.m.) The result was that attendance at the vespers increased perceptibly and the nine o'clock fellowship hour programs began to grow in great numbers. At the present time, the attendance at Sunday Evening Vespers runs about three hundred and fifty, but may, at times, reach as high as a thousand or more. Attendance at the Fellowship Hour programs will average close to three hundred, and often the Fellowship Hall is packed and ' standing.' Special programs have, on occasion, forced moving back into the sanctuary because of the crowds.

"In 1965, the young adults asked if they might stay on after the Fellowship Hour program. With approval of the deacons, the "Coffee House" was initiated from 10 to 12 p.m. in the Youth Hall. For the most part, this period was simply a relaxed group of young adults gathering to visit, have an extra cup of coffee, and occasionally enjoy a sing-along.

"About 90 percent of those who attend the vesper service are young adults (18-35), and the usual crowd at the nine o'clock program is at least 90 percent young adults. Most of them are not members of Central, and many are not Lutheran. They come from the Twin Cities and many surrounding communities."

Winter was coming on, but thoughts of the coming summer already were entering the minds of many of Central's members, especially those who had taken part in the camp program during the season that had ended a short time before. With this in mind, a special appeal during the year's Every Member Canvass for contributions to the Minneapolis circuit ELC Bible camp at Clearwater Lake was made. Earnest solicitors were able to show that although the camp had been in operation only one year, four hundred and three campers had been accommodated there, in addition to weekend retreats and special conferences. The sum of $8,000 was pledged during the canvass, which added to the balance of $4,000 in the camp treasury, assured another successful year of camp activities during the following summer.

The spiritual overtones of events at home and abroad began to be reviewed by Pastor Gornitzka over radio station WCCO at this time. A trial period of several months was set to try out the experiment. A broadcast five minutes in length was made each weekday from Monday through Friday immediately following the popular Cedric Adams newscast at 10:15 p.m. The first broadcast of the series was made on November 12. Each broadcast originated in either the parsonage study or the radio station.

"Central Lutheran feels honored in Pastor Gornitzka having been asked to produce this program," said Leif R. Larson, the church's executive secretary. "You are asked to take advantage of the thought-provoking comments on the news as it is reviewed by our pastor."

A proposal was made by the Lutheran Welfare Society of Minnesota to erect an administrative headquarters building to take care of its many statewide projects. A site at 2400 Park Avenue in Minneapolis was bought and plans were made to construct the building. True to its tradition of helpfulness, Central Lutheran Church pledged the sum of $7,200 toward the estimated cost. Special contributions by its members were encouraged. In his appeal to the Lutherans of the state, the Rev. Luthard Gjerde, executive secretary of the society, said, "Lutheran churches are working together in warmhearted Christian compassion in meeting the needs of helpless children and troubled people. The ways in which they work are many, helping to encircle the changeless Cross of Christ. This building will be an outlet for welfare services to those in need."

The members of Central were eager to have a part in this worthy endeavor and pledged their support of the project.

With a vision of long-range planning, the program of land acquisition, started back in 1948, continued on through the Hjortland pastorate. Being aware of the ever-growing need for additional parking facilities, the Board of Trustees purchased more land during the period from 1956 to 1966. With the development of the freeway into the loop area, it became imperative that 1,000 parking spaces be made available for the worshippers at the church services. This objective is soon to be accomplished.

An event with a worldwide impact with Central as its focal point took place in the summer of 1957. The third assembly of the Lutheran World Federation met in Minneapolis for eleven days, from August 15th through the 25th. More than 50,000 Lutherans from 62 countries gathered here for the largest and most significant assembly ever to convene in this country. Those who gathered together in this vast assembly represented the 70,000,000 Lutherans of the world, this church being the largest of all Protestant denominations.

Included among the overseas delegations were presidents, premiers and vice premiers of several European, African and Asian countries, as well as bishops, pastors, professors, judges, special ambassadors, deacons and deaconesses, housewives and other representatives from all walks of life. Visas were granted to some from behind the Iron Curtain, to add their worth to that of their fellow members from the free nations of the world.

Minneapolis was chosen as the site for the assembly because it was the center of a vast Lutheran population. It was estimated that over two million of America's seven million Lutherans lived in the immediate five-state area. Just as Minneapolis was the center of Lutheranism is our country, so was Central Church the center of this denomination in the city in which it was located.

"Ours is a great privilege and a tremendous task," said Pastor Gornitzka, commenting on the World Wide Assembly. "This is far more than a gathering of thousands of people from all corners of the world. It is a praying, planning, thinking, speaking assembly gathered here to concern themselves with great issues confronting the church of Jesus Christ in our day. The central theme is 'Christ Frees and Unites.' Whatever is ours to share in loving service, let us share it."

Delegates who marched in the opening procession assembled in the sanctuary of Central Lutheran. Part of the overflow crowd which could not get into the municipal auditorium heard the opening service piped into Central Lutheran Church. Each morning of the assembly, Central provided a service of Holy Communion open to the delegates and visitors. Official delegates and visitors were served their meals at Central. Several of the assembly discussion groups convened in Central's parish house.

On the evening of August 15, 1957, Bishop Lajos Ordass, leader of the Hungarian Lutheran Church, spoke to the assembled delegates in the Minneapolis municipal auditorium, keynoting the convention. His message brought to the minds of the thousands of listeners the fateful years that Bishop Ordass had lived since the first similar assembly in Lund, Sweden, ten years previously. There were many who recalled his deposition from office and subsequent imprisonment under false charges of the Communist Kadar regime. They remembered, too, the scoffing words which greeted the attempt on the part of Bishop Lilje, Federation president, and Carl Lund-Quist, executive secretary, to secure Ordass' freedom.

"We don't fear the Lutheran Church," the Communists said. "It is nothing but old people about to die. We have the youth."

The fateful uprisings against the Communist regime which followed soon after this were not by the despised old people of Hungary, but by the youth, those whom the Communist leaders had boasted were on their side.

"There is freedom in Hungary today, and unity," declared Bishop Ordass, "but not of the material, earthly kind. It is the freedom and the unity that are found only in Christ."

It was a comparison not soon forgotten by the assembled delegates.

"Central," said Dr. Carl E. Lund-Quist, Lutheran World Federation executive secretary, after the assembly, "becomes a symbol of what the Minneapolis assembly will mean in Lutheran Church history. The way in which you placed these facilities at our disposal and the excellent cooperation of pastors and members will long be affectionately remembered."

Central's new parish house was completed during the summer and dedication services were held on August 4. The rite of dedication, performed by Dr. E. C. Reinertson, president of the ELC Southern District, took place before the main entrance to the new structure. Guest speaker at the two morning services was Dr. Elmer Hjortland, former pastor of Central. It was during his ministry that this parish unit was visualized and a building fund was created to fulfill the plans.

With the completion of the new parish house, a new service was added to the already extensive list of ways in which Central reached into the lives of its members. A portion of the new structure was set aside to be used as a combination library and bookstore, professionally planned and operated. It had a threefold purpose: to aid in the educational program of the church; to be of service to the organizations of Central, and to serve as a source of good literature for the congregation. Selected to serve as volunteer librarian was Miss Ellen Ulland, who devoted many hours to establishing the library and store. Funds to make this service possible came from contributions by individuals. A large gift made by one member enabled Miss Ulland to open the department with well-stocked shelves on November 22, 1957. In another month, a lending library was started to enlarge the service to members.

Impressed by the possibilities offered by this division of the church, the Board of Trustees decided to provide for its future by setting aside each year a specific sum in the budget. Contributions were also welcomed from the organizations of the church. Memorial funds and bookstore sales added to the funds available. Books for all ages were placed on the shelves for sale: preschool and grade school level, teen-age level, books for laymen, Christian educators, devotional literature, doctrinal material, religious publications and mental health books.

The library was located strategically on the main floor of the north wing of the parish house just inside the main entrance. The architects planned this room to be conspicuously open to view, with shelves on two walls and open grillwork on the other two. Operating with the library was the bookstore where not only publications, but also religious gift items and stationery supplies were placed on sale. Opened twenty-one years ago, this department has achieved its purpose well. Since Miss Ulland's death, several volunteers have continued her unselfish services. It is another example of the spirit that has made Central Lutheran the "Miracle Church."

More and more attention was being given to extending the activities of the Pastor's Cabinet. Local district leaders were continuing to visit Central's members in their areas, to report back to the church office anything they discovered needing pastoral help, and to contact prospects for church membership. In March 1957, a committee to evaluate the program was selected and a decision was made to give it added significance by placing a pastor in charge. The Rev. Dennis Griffin was selected to supervise this important activity under a new name of the Life and Growth Planning Committee on August 1, 1958, and he continued for 30 months to direct 150 members in this personal evangelistic program. In September 1961, the Rev. Owen E. Doely joined the staff and continued to direct the Life and Growth program.

It is important to realize how necessary the Pastor's Cabinet and the Life and Growth Committee have been when you understand that Central's membership is not static. On the fifteenth anniversary of the founding of the church, Dr. Stub announced from the pulpit that 7,000 members had come and gone during that period. This changing membership has continued up to the present time. In 1968, there were 445 accessions of members and 394 separations. This is an annual experience. Why?

It has been said that Central Lutheran Church represents the "threshold of Lutheranism" in Minneapolis. Over the years as individuals came to the city to work and to live, they settled in the inner city. It was logical for them to join a Lutheran church within close proximity. Later, as they bought a home and moved into the suburbs, it was logical, too, that they join a neighborhood church. It was more convenient; it was easier to get their children to Sunday school. Perhaps in the future this situation may be altered because of the easy new freeway access to Central Lutheran Church.

The challenge of the future is anticipated by one phase of the Life and Growth Committee as given by Pastor

Dr. J. A. O. Stub

Dr. E. S. Hjortland

Pastor Reinholtzen, Dr. Hjortland, Pastor Maynard Iverson

Leif R. Larson

Dr. A. Reuben Gornitzka

Pastor Scheie, Dr. Gornitzka, Pastor Thompson, Pastor Doely

Dr. Morris Wee

Hoover T. Grimsby

Doely in his annual report to the congregation for 1968: "Another new program which was initiated in 1967 under the leadership of Life and Growth couples was the 'Sponsorship' plan. This means that each individual or couple that joins Central will have a 'special introducer' and friend who is already an active member of Central. The role of the sponsor is to help the new member become acquainted with all the opportunities of membership through fellowship, personal growth and service. It is a relationship that lasts formally for one year and will build a strong bond of friendship between members. I believe that it is one of the most thrilling and satisfying programs that has been brought into the life of Central recently. It augments the fine work which is done by Neighborhood Leaders to integrate new members into the adventure of being a member of Central Lutheran Church.

"We have had record attendance at the Adult Inquiry classes in 1968, and this reflects the faithful and dedicated calling which our Mission of the Seventy lay visitors have done to promote interest in this 'Open Door' into life in the church. New member prospects and general prospects are contacted by these Central Lutheran Church members. They call at their homes to personally confront them with the exciting possibilities of the Christian life and membership at Central."

Here is another evidence of the active participation of the lay members of Central in fulfilling its mission as a servant church, and to underscore its potential for the future.

It was in 1958 that a unique committee was appointed at Central, the influence of which made itself felt throughout the church and the community that it served. It was given the name of the "Forward Planning Committee." It was composed of people who had had experience in the various areas of activity within the church. It was the objective of the committee to make a thorough study of each of these areas and to analyze the findings for the purpose of determining the nature of improvements which could be made.

The mission of Central Lutheran Church was outlined by Dr. Gornitzka for the committee: "Time and space does not permit me to indicate in detail the many avenues we travel in order to achieve what we believe to be God's purpose for us here.

"Involved in the scope of our congregation's total ministry and concern are the frustrated, lost, and lonely, in miserable and overcrowded rooms on shabby streets; the defeated and despairing newcomers to the city who have made wrong choices and seek the healing and forgiving love of Christ; the tense and fearful who wrestle with a strongly competitive society in the world of business and industry; the sick on a white-sheeted hospital bed; the sorrowing at a graveside; the doubting who seek to know and be sure; the radio listener with a hungry ear for the voice of God amidst the clamoring voices of men; the community with its need for a leaven, a salt, and a light in the midst of a too secularized and materialistic society; the church at large, which is but an extension of all congregational arms, our own included.

"And because this is true, we can rededicate ourselves to our task and accept even blindly the promise that God will do even more than we ask or dare to think."

As a topic was chosen, it was studied intensively in an attempt to discover solutions to existing problems.

Constructive suggestions which resulted were presented to the proper board or to the church council for consideration and possible development. There was one program which the committee took upon itself to develop and that was the leaders' planning conference. At the first session, reports were heard on each area of congregational life, and plans were made for the coming year. So successful were the initial sessions that they were made an annual event.

One of the conclusions reached by the group of earnest workers was that the very heart of their congregational life was the Sunday worship service. There was no other time or place when the whole congregation came together regularly with but one purpose in mind — that of glorifying God. Sermon, hymn and liturgy combined to unite the worshippers in a common bond of faith.

However, it was realized that worship did not end with the Sunday service, but that personal and family worship were of importance to the spiritual welfare of the individual members of the congregation. It was to aid in this significant work of the church that devotional booklets were given to each family, together with tracts and other helpful materials. Not only was regular attendance at worship stressed, but added importance was given to participation in the sacrament of Holy Communion. It was decided that this significant sacrament was to be celebrated regularly on the first and third Sundays of each month. Regular attendance at both worship and Communion heightened the interest of the members in their church and deepened their conception of what it meant to them individually to be a member of Central's family of worshippers.

The situation with American Indians who had moved into the city from their reservations provided a serious problem for Minneapolis. Many had been placed on public welfare and were living in submarginal circumstances. Aware of their plight, Central Lutheran Church, true to its mission as a servant church, volunteered to help by offering free office space for the director of the city-wide project in 1962, which continued for three years. This is just another example of Central's participation in solving community problems.

Special consideration was given to the study of summer activities of Central. There was a tendency in many churches to "let down" during the summer months. However, the feeling at Central Lutheran was that the summer season was especially suited to participation in many activities that were more difficult to take part in during less favorable times of the year. The result was a stepped-up program of activities, rather than a modified one. A vacation Bible school was organized, with sessions held daily. On the evening of the final day, a special program was staged by the various departments of the school, with all members of the church, and especially all parents, invited to attend.

The success of the Bible Camp at Clearwater previously assured an enriched program again this year, and registration was higher than it had been the year before. Sunday School classes met on schedule, including a chapel period for all, featuring common worship and hymn singing. New to this year's summer schedule for youth was a series of guided services for youth, including trips to the air base, the Ford plant, the

Como Park zoo, the state capitol building, the Mayo Clinic in Rochester, the famed Crystal cave, and the Dalles of the St. Croix. The intriguing title of "Central Lutheran Adventure Club" was given to the group of young people who signed up for the tours.

In these many ways did the members of Central seek to build up interest in their church's goals rather than to have them wither and perhaps die through inactivity.

When in September 1958, the pastors, church staff, presidents or chairmen of the church boards and organizations met at a retreat at Grand View Lodge on Gull Lake in northern Minnesota to review the activities of the year, it was with a strong feeling of satisfaction that they looked back upon the immediate past. It had been a full year, with a strong program to complete it. Spiritual strength had suffered no diminution at Central Lutheran this year.

It was an impressive list of achievements that were credited to the church and its organizations at the end of this year of special effort. Outlined in a report given at a leaders' conference were:

• Addition to the staff of a pastor for Life and Growth and the expansion of this congregational program.

• Expansion of a social welfare service through the development of home service workers, service to institutions and care of the needy under the direction of the parish social worker.

• Expansion of the adult education program, with several additional classes added.

• Addition of a communion service on the third Sunday of each month with a resulting increase in communion attendance.

- Staff addition of an intern through a Rockefeller grant.

- Purchase of additional buildings in the immediate area of the church and their demolition to provide for badly needed parking space. Plans were made to purchase, in the future, all structures in the church block in order to provide additional space.

- More effective use of volunteers throughout the church through the work of the parish services director.

- Organization of the Luther League into teams according to areas similar to the Life and Growth plan.

- Initial contributions by organizations to scholarships for youth summer camps and conferences.

- Increased visitation by groups in cooperation with the staff.

- Greater interest in and support of missionary activities by groups.

- Development of the Little Singers of Central and participation by hundreds of singers in the musical program of the church.

- Organization by the new Flower and Decorating Committee of a flower calendar.

It was good to look back and to count the blessings of a year gone by. It was challenging to look ahead and to plan the goals for a year yet unborn. In the autumn workshop, anticipating the labors of the coming year, new goals were set. When they were completed, the list was an impressive one. These were the goals sought for the coming church year:

- Expansion of the youth program under a full-time youth director.

- Study of acquisition of additional parking area and the construction of a chapel.

- Increased membership in organizations.

- Development of an effective visitation program by organizations.

- Through the Life and Growth program, increased Sunday School enrollment in order to make full use of available space. Development of transportation service for youth and the aged.

- Encouragement to organizations to assist in the welfare work of the church.

- Establishment of committees to study housing for the aged and expansion of clinical counseling services.

- Study of present membership voting procedure.

- Promotion of membership in the blood donors group.

- Reevaluation and study of professional staff positions to insure the best possible service and efficiency.

- Plan a more complete adult education program.

- Implementation in every way of a Life and Growth program.

- Extension of the present Bible study program.

Sixty years had now gone by since Central first opened its doors. It began with vigor, ambitious to carry out its planned program of service. Threescore years had witnessed no lessening of the faith that the founders had in their church. Rather, at the end of this long period of time the work was still going on, stronger, sturdier than at its inception, with the eyes of the workers directed to the future. Central Lutheran drew no bounds to circumscribe its vision.

The original organ, by 1960, was worn out and needed to be replaced. A committee was appointed in 1961 to make a survey of suitable instruments and recommended the purchase of a Cassavant organ in January 1962. To install it would require remodeling the chancel. The congregation approved the recommendation at a total cost of approximately $225,000. The installation was completed in March 1963, and dedicated on April 19, 1964. Thus another milestone was reached in improving the worship services of Central.

The Altar Guild, organized in 1958, has a large corps of women to assist in the total program of the chancel, chapels and communion. They assist the deacons on Sacramental Sunday and other communion services. They maintain in proper order and repair the altar hanging, linens, towels, and other articles. In 1968, the Sewing Guild made 1546 baptismal towels which were hemmed and embroidered with a white satin stitched cross, totaling 4638 hours of labor. Children and adults receive the towels used at their baptism. The work of this organization is another example of the manner in which members of the congregation participate in the everyday affairs of the church.

It was during the Easter season in the year 1919 that Central Lutheran Church began its long life of service. It had prospered and grown far beyond the hopes of its founders. The leadership that had been provided by the senior pastors had been of the highest order. For a quarter of a century, Dr. Stub had headed the staff, followed by the Rev. Hjortland. He in turn had been succeeded by the Rev. Reuben Gornitzka. Now it was the senior pastor's wish to go elsewhere, a decision that saddened the people of Central. His farewell sermon was preached on Easter Sunday, 1963. Another phase of Central's history had ended. A new one was about to begin.

CHAPTER **11**

A Bright New Era Begins for Central

"All of good the past hath had remains to make our own time glad." — Whittier

As an expression of gratitude for Dr. Gornitzka's participation in civic activities and serving on important committees, particularly the Municipal Auditorium building committee, a city-wide testimonial dinner was sponsored by several members of the City Council, the Downtown Council, the Chamber of Commerce, officials of organized labor and other civic organizations on April 16, 1963. Almost a thousand citizens were in attendance to demonstrate their appreciation to one who has meant so much to the community.

"My new work will be principally a special ministry, nationally, in business, industrial and entertainment fields. I will speak at conferences and conventions and at times confer confidentially with individuals in these areas of American life. I shall also do some writing and, on occasion, some radio and television work." Thus did the departing pastor of Central Lutheran Church explain the work that he had elected to do in the future as the Executive Director of Direction, Inc.

How does a church with a history of greatness proceed with the selection of a senior pastor when a vacancy occurs, as it did in the spring of the year 1963?

As it had done in the past on three occasions, it first surveyed the field of pastors who were already known to Central. Among those looked upon with favor was the Rev. Dr. Morris Wee, who had been pastor of Bethel Lutheran Church in Madison, Wisconsin, for twenty-three years. For three years he had been president of Carthage College in Illinois, three years the pastor of First Lutheran Church in Duluth, and for three years the Executive Director of the Division of Student Service of the National Lutheran Council. With this background of experience he was eminently qualified to become the senior pastor of Central Lutheran Church.

Dr. Wee had filled the pulpit at Central on special occasions and the congregation remembered him with much favor. He was 57 years old, a native Minnesotan, and the holder of a Ph.D. degree in history from the University of Wisconsin.

It was decided to issue a call to Dr. Wee, which the Central congregation did in the late spring following Dr. Gornitzka's farewell sermon. Dr. Wee's acceptance of the call was announced to the congregation on May 26. In his letter of acceptance, he said, "Even as Central Lutheran congregation believed it was led by God to extend the call to me, I am confident that God has guided me to accept it."

Before assuming his duties at Central, Dr. Wee left for a month's vacation trip to northern Europe. Included on the itinerary was attendance at the Lutheran World Federation Assembly in Helsinki, Finland. His first sermon was preached at Central on September 22, 1963; installation was set for October 13. Assisting at the installation ceremony was Dr. Fredrik Schiotz, president of the American Lutheran Church and newly elected president of the Lutheran World Federation. The sermon that day was preached by Dr. Melford Knutson, district president of the Southeastern Minnesota District of the American Lutheran Church.

Once again a bright new era was about to begin for Central.

Several months after his installation as senior pastor, Dr. Wee was able to say: "It is exciting to be a member of Central Lutheran Church. There are so many things happening here that one cannot help but be excited. The new pipe organ is almost completed, with its 6,000 pipes tuned to perfection. The new altar hangings have added freshness and color to the chancel of the church. Two new staff members have been added; the youth groups are busy with ambitious programs; 'Sunday Evening at Central' continues to grow; the music is superb; the missionary program is strong and vigorous . . . Every week brings new surprises. My respect for the congregation members grows and grows. God love you always and keep you in His care." Thus did the spirit of Central descend upon the new pastor.

A program pioneered by Central was begun during the year 1964. It concerned a leave-of-absence plan for its ministers. Three years before this the official boards of the congregation began a study of plans which would have as their objective providing additional opportunity for its ministers to travel and undertake special study. The conviction had grown strong that with the very busy schedule which the pastors had at Central, it would be imperative that extra time should be found for these purposes. In 1963, a plan was adopted whereby a pastor who had served Central for at least three years might submit a proposal to the Board of Deacons for special study. If the proposal was accepted, the pastor could be granted up to two months for the purpose proposed.

The first pastor to be given such a leave of absence was Pastor Scheie. His proposal was that he make a special study of the ministry to the sick and shut-ins as it was carried out in several selected congregations. In addition, he proposed to attend a seminar for pastors at a West Coast theological seminary as well as to be present at several summer religious conferences. The Board of Deacons approved his request and his sabbatical was taken in the summer of 1964.

It was in the autumn of this year that Central observed the 45th anniversary of its founding. The anniversary Sunday was October 18, a day dedicated to a renewal of the purposes stated by Pastor Stub in the year 1919:

"The church must strive to be a real church home for people of all conditions and ages. It must teem with activity. Its doors must be open in welcome to all, irrespective of antecedents or social position. It must be our Father's house, where all can feel at home. In other words, the church does not exist so much for its members as it does for the opportunity that it gives them to serve the Lord."

Dr. Elmer S. Hjortland, Central's second senior pastor and minister for the ten years from 1945 to 1955, preached the anniversary sermons that day to capacity crowds. In the evening a reception was held for Central's former pastor and his wife, with coffee served in the lounge until midnight.

When the every-member canvass was made in October and November 1964, the theme adopted was "Central Lutheran — A Servant Church." A booklet was prepared for distribution not only to members, but to thousands of others as well, stressing this theme as the real image of Central. To support this servant church, dedicated members made their pledges in advance, but it was pointed out that a large percentage of those in attendance at Sunday services at Central were visitors. To pinpoint the issue, a poll was taken one Sunday which showed that 38 percent of those present were visitors.

When stewardship dinners were held, Dr. Wee took as his topic the same theme that was carried through the entire anniversary period. Over 300 workers made personal calls on those who did not attend the dinners. A budget of $475,000 was approved, $315,000 of which was expected to be pledged, with approximately $175,000 additional coming from gifts, collections, and other sources.

When the campaign ended, the amount pledged was found to exceed the estimate, the average pledge being $126 for the year or $2.43 per Sunday. This figure set a new record for Central.

A little-known activity at Central that had for its purpose service to the children of the community was begun in 1962. It was the Saturday Neighborhood Library Hour. Sponsored by the library committee, the intent of this hour was to open the facilities of Central's children's library to children of the neighborhood. A year after it began, there were forty children enrolled. No fee was charged. The group met between 9:30 and 11 a.m. on Saturday, with an average attendance of more than twenty. Most of the children were from nonmember homes, and many of them were from unchurched homes.

A typical library hour included time for browsing, story-reading-time activities, and crafts. Milk and cookies were served for refreshments. Often the hour was closed with the showing of a short Bible story film or filmstrip. The volunteer teachers soon found that many of the children like to come early — and stay late.

Another of the services offered by Central was the reception service for weddings, anniversaries, and other special occasions. These services had been provided by the church for many years, but as time passed they tended to become increasingly specialized and apart from the luncheons and dinner occasions that occurred regularly in the course of the year. Once under the direction of the Day Guild, for several years it had been supervised by the head of the food service, Mrs. Gertrude Frisch, who has since retired.

"I would not begin to handle the many receptions without the help of volunteers," said Mrs. Frisch. "Many of the women who help have their own white uniforms and really enjoy the work that they do. This service has become an integral part of our church's program."

One of the women is designated to serve as the wedding hostess. Since the wedding day is one of the loveliest and most memorable days in the lives of the bride and groom, the wedding hostess aids in every way possible, reviewing each detail of the wedding service. Along with the pastor and the organist, the wedding hostess attends each rehearsal. She lends a helping hand with the arrangements at the altar and assists with details of the processional and recessional. She shows the bride to the bride's room and helps her and her attendants with the gowns that are to be worn during the ceremony. If the wedding reception is to be held at the church, the hostess assists with the formation of the reception line and with other details.

Before the ceremony begins, she makes a final check. Does everyone have a boutonniere or a corsage? Have arrangements been made for the picture taking? Is the guest book ready, with someone in charge? Are all the men in the sacristy who are to take part? Are the ushers ready? It is the wedding hostess who gives the signals for the procession to begin. After the ceremony ends, there are many additional details to take care of.

It is interesting to note that at the 45th annual meeting of the congregation that was held on January 26, 1965, plans were already being made for observing the 50th anniversary of the founding of Central Lutheran. At that time it was noted by several members that the year 1969 was still quite some distance in the future, but the consensus of the group was that it was not too early to begin planning.

Reports at this annual meeting in 1965 revealed the fact that the total endowment funds of the church had reached an impressive total of $608,866, an increase of $43,764 over the previous year's figure. Of this figure, $36,818 was received from the estates of several members of Central who had died during the year. An additional $12,140 was received in the form of memorials and other gifts.

An event of more than usual interest took place on May 16, 1965, when an organ and choir festival was held at Central in honor of the 90th birthday of Dr. Albert Schweitzer. A performance of the complete "Messiah" was given by the Senior Choir and the Minneapolis Symphony musicians. On the next two days, an organ symposium and an all-Bach program were given. The music committee worked with the church boards on the plans. The festival was initiated by the Friends of Albert Schweitzer, a Boston organization. Said Frederic Hilary, Central's minister of music, "Our congregation is honored to receive this invitation. The music department and the music committee have worked strenuously for many weeks to make this occasion memorable. Albert Schweitzer was the first crusader for the return of the golden age of organ building. He is perhaps the leading authority of this generation on the music of Bach."

When the Hilarys joined the staff in 1954, a new impetus was given to the music program of Central. "Christmas at Central" has been presented annually. Berlioz' "Te Deum" was translated from the Latin into English by Frederic Hilary, and the combined choirs gave the first performance of it in America in 1957. A repeat performance was given in August when it was recorded and long-playing records were offered for sale. It was presented again in March 1958. Over the years there have been presentations of Beethoven's "Missa Solemnis," Bruckner's "Mass in F Minor," Berlioz' "Requiem," and several presentations of Handel's "Messiah."

Dr. Elmer Hjortland, who was instrumental in getting the Hilarys to join the staff at Central, has commented: "Fred's ability as a director and his fine appreciation of church music is, I think, most unusual and, of course, the buoyant spirit of Joyce and her remarkable interpretation of organ music makes them a prize pair at Central."

The overall program of the music department of Central was outlined by Mr. Hilary in his report to the congregation at its annual meeting in January 1969:

"The music program at Central Lutheran Church is built on a multiple choir organization, choirs of all ages from first grade up through adulthood. All participants are volunteer singers. This program is becoming rare in the inner-city, downtown church, where many examples of professionalism have invaded and harmed the true service-oriented music-worship program.

"Central has unique opportunities for service in four areas, all related to music and worship:

"First — Participation. People of all ages can find an opportunity to serve their church in its worship services, according to their various talents, and to learn and sing the great choral music of the Christian tradition.

"Second — Education. For the young people this is their first training in responsibility and regularity, so helpful both to themselves and to the church. While developing poise as representatives of their church, they also learn the Lutheran liturgies, hymns and larger sacred works. Whenever possible, the younger groups are combined with the older to experience the unusual sacred works that would be too difficult for them to perform alone.

"Third — Group Discipline. The learning and performing of the most difficult anthems and larger

138

choral works require a working together in fellowship, and a discipline of merging the individual self into a larger group organization that brings out talents beyond one's own particular limitations. This brings about close ties of friendship, and a family closeness, that becomes a vital part of our larger family at Central Lutheran Church. At times as many as four or five members of one family are all members of various choirs.

"*Fourth — the Outreach.* The music of the church should reach out to the neighborhood and community. The thousands of visitors to our church at services and special concerts are supplemented by the groups which make our church a special point of interest on 'field trips.' This includes schools and other churches. Our 'new' Cassavant organ is a special point of interest to these groups as well as the weekly 'tour groups' on Sunday mornings that ask for organ demonstrations. Another dimension has been added during the last five years, an annual 'Organ Symposium', attracting over 100 participants for two days of lectures on the latest developments in organ construction and performance. Outstanding organists from America and Europe are brought to Minneapolis for organ recitals during the year.

"Special events of this past year included concerts and lectures by world-famous authorities and performing artists during the annual Organ and Choral Festival in the spring. In October 1968, there was a special organ recital by Joyce Hilary.

"The Senior Choir embarked on its most ambitious undertaking to date when it presented the Bach St. John Passion, with guest soloists and members of the Minneapolis Symphony Orchestra. This was performed

139

on Monday of 'Holy Week,' 1968. The choirs combined in the annual 'Christmas at Central' on December 15, 1968. The theme, relating the birth of the Christ child to contemporary times, was entitled 'The Birth of a Child — the Worth of a Man.'"

The Visitation Pastor, L. F. Scheie, has reported on his work: "There is a certain sameness in the visitation ministry to the sick and shut-ins from year to year. Sickness and infirmity continue in our midst and bring with them the same consequences of inconvenience, loneliness, heartache, suffering, frustration and sorrow. But then there is also the wonderful gospel of hope, of peace, of power with which to face these besetting problems. Our privilege of sharing that gospel with all we can reach, also remains the same. This, however, in no way makes this ministry an uninteresting one.

"There are new people to minister to continually. It is not only gives us opportunity to get to know the members of Central better, but also to reach others — members of other congregations, and often those who are not affiliated with any church. It is a real joy to discover again and again that the members of Central have been wonderful witnesses to those whom they have met because of a hospital or nursing home confinement or visit."

At this time an incident occurred that brought home to Dr. Wee the need for a new program. One day he visited a home for elderly people and asked for a certain man who resided there. The girl at the desk said that he was in and then added. "He is terribly lonely. His days are long, with no place to go and few people come to see him."

"There must be many lonely people like him," observed Pastor Wee. "They need love more than they need bread. Central's members are going to give them a new and substantial measure of concern."

Soon a large group of volunteers was being recruited, to be friends of the lonely one. Each Friendly Visitor was asked to "adopt" one elderly or shut-in person and to make that individual a matter of personal concern. The visitor was requested to call on his new friend at least once every other week and to do as many helpful acts as he is able to do.

Mrs. Elmer M. Rusten, chairman of the Friendly Visitors Committee, has reported that a total of 140 assigned visitors made a total of 2,280 calls on shut-ins during 1968 to assist in meeting their physical, social and spiritual needs. At Easter and Christmas the committee helped in the planning and distribution of the chancel plants to shut-ins as follows: 205 Easter lilies and 137 poinsettias.

Many an elderly person who had wondered if anyone really cared was made happy again. This was another example of the type of service that Central has always been ready to perform, looking to the welfare and happiness of others.

The continuing program of helping the unfortunate has continued through the years in spite of present-day welfare programs. The Rev. Orin Thompson reports on Central's welfare service:

"An inner-city church like Central is confronted daily by the needs of various people who enter our doors. Many are transients, passing through the city. Others are from our own neighborhood. Each person who comes is interviewed by one of the pastors in an effort to understand the particular problem involved. The doors are closed to no one. However, occasionally requests may be denied if the requests are unreasonable, or it is determined that needs represented are not legitimate. Most common is the request for meals or food, in which instances a modest grocery order may be given. Other needs that are common are for lodging, and rooms may be provided in inexpensive hotels. Clothing which has been donated by members of the congregation is also given to individuals and occasionally to needy families. Experience has demonstrated the wisdom of giving help in kind rather than in cash.

"In most instances the immediate needs for food, etc., are only the evidence of deeper and more complex personal and family problems, in which case the pastors will seek to give help and counsel. Often the help needed may be given by referring the individual to community and welfare agencies which offer assitance. They may be referred to the Community Welfare and Referral Service, Travelers' Aid, AA, etc. Chaplains of both juvenile and adult courts make frequent referrals to the pastors of Central."

Another matter of concern that was brought to the attention of Central's members at this time pertained to scholarships and the Central Lutheran Church Foundation. It was recognized that scholarships or grants-in-aid to worthy and needy students had become increasingly necessary as college costs soared higher and higher.

"If we are able to invest some of our dollars in human resources, we are doing a good thing," observed Dr. Wee. "The young people at Central are about the most valuable human resources that I can think of. This congregation has a special foundation to receive gifts of money or property called the Central Lutheran Church Foundation. Gifts given to it are kept in perpetuity and only the interest earned is used for church purposes. The fund itself remains intact. Here is an excellent way in which to strengthen the hands of Central for the future. Scholarships and the Central Foundation — two wonderful ways by which much good can be done."

It will be recalled that during the early years of Central and also in the hard years of the depression, tickets to church dinners sold for 50 cents or even 35 cents. Gradually, with a rising economy and higher prices for commodities, the ticket costs rose bit by bit. They were an accurate barometer of the economic condition of the country. A note in the April 1964 issue of the *Spirit of Central* reflects the inflation that took place in the 1960's: "The annual Sweethearts' Banquet of the Men of Central will be held on Thursday, April 29. Featured as speaker will be Dr. E. S. Hjortland, former senior pastor of Central. Mrs. Hjortland will also be in attendance. The cost of the tickets will be $3.50 per couple. Dinner will be served at 6:30 p.m."

Before the decade ended, tickets for dinners would be considered reasonably priced at this cost for each one. The price per plate for the Fiftieth Anniversary Banquet was $6.00.

For many years, Central had been interested in the Ebenezer Home, operated by the Ebenezer Home Society, a nonprofit organization owned and operated by affiliated congregations of the American Lutheran Church in Hennepin County. It provided total care —

143

that is, all types of services — for older men and women. It had been in operation since 1917, two years before Central was founded. The goal of the home was to assist persons in this age group to solve their problems, whether they were personal, physical, financial, legal or spiritual. In 1964, there were 385 residents in the home. Almost half of them were receiving nursing care. A staff of 75 nurses and nurses aides looked after the needs of these patients. A medical staff of 17 doctors was provided, and two full-time chaplains looked after the spiritual needs of the residents. In 1979, 56 of the men and women residing at the Ebenezer Home were members of Central Lutheran.

One of the goals in Central's building program was the erection of a chapel, to become a part of Greater Central. At the annual meeting, held on January 25, 1966, Dr. Wee recommended that the church trustees should proceed immediately with plans for the construction of the chapel. In addition, the trustees were instructed to secure professional assistance in formulating plans for Central City. There was unanimous action taken on the two recommendations by the congregation. At the April meeting of the Board of Trustees, it was voted to proceed with the chapel construction, as the third unit of the Greater Central program, begun in 1951. Walter F. MacGregor, architect for the parish house and preliminary plans for the chapel, was granted continuance of his contract. Working closely with him were members of the chapel committee, Dr. Wee, and the church business administrator. But these plans did not materialize. It was decided to wait until the program of land acquisition was completed when a more suitable site would be available.

Central Lutheran was one of the first churches of the American Lutheran group to employ a professional business administrator. This was in 1950. The man selected for this important post was Leif R. Larson, former YMCA secretary. For sixteen years he served in this capacity, making his term of service the second longest career of professional service in Central's history. Only Pastor Stub served longer. On June 1, 1966, he retired, bringing to a close a period of service that was marked with signal success. During the sixteen years that he guided the business affairs of Central, growth marked every phase of the church's activities. Membership rose from 4,142 to 5,709; canvass pledges increased from $142,000 to $340,000; expenditures experienced a similar increase, from $151,075 to $508,129. Two units of the parish house were constructed during these years, a new organ was installed and the chancel was remodeled. There were no parking facilities in 1950; in 1966 there were five lots with facilities for 375 cars.

In 1973 Clayton G. Spranger became the business administrator of Central after serving for ten years in a similar position at Ascension Lutheran Church in Milwaukee. He has been president of the National Association of Business Administrators.

An unusual situtation developed at Central when Dr. Wee was asked by the officials of the American Lutheran Church to serve for one year as national chairman for a special fund-raising project. The purpose of the drive was to raise $20,000,000 for American Lutheran Church colleges and schools. The Central congregation agreed to "loan" their senior pastor to the national organization for the year as requested. The Rev. J. N. Quello, senior pastor of the First Lutheran Church of Fargo, North Dakota, was extended a call to serve as Central's associate pastor during the year. Dr. Wee retained his position as senior pastor with Dr. Quello filling the pulpit and assuming the senior pastor's duties when occasion required. On Thanksgiving Day, 1967, his mission completed, Dr. Wee again assumed his full duties at Central. It had been a rewarding year for him and for the American Lutheran Church.

March 23, 1967, was a significant day for Central Lutheran. On that day articles of incorporation were drawn up for the Camp Amnicon Foundation.

It was in the summer of 1966 that Mr. and Mrs. Martin Burtness of Superior, Wisconsin, donated forty-five acres of land to Central Lutheran Church. This property was given for the express purpose of developing a camp, not only for the children, but also for the adult members of the congregation. It was located at the very end of Moccasin-Mike road, fifteen miles east of Superior, where the Amnicon River emptied into Lake Superior. When the land was given to Central, there was no development of any kind on it. In fact, there wasn't even a road leading into it.

During the year, plans were made looking toward the development of a congregational camp on the wild land. A board of directors was chosen and the camp was incorporated as a separate nonprofit entity, solely owned and operated by Central. Additional land was purchased south of the first tract, providing a total of eighty-five acres of wild Wisconsin land as a nucleus for the camp that as yet existed only on paper. In order to help many people to visualize the dream that the camp's founders shared, during the summer of 1967 arrangements were made for many members of Central's congregation to visit the site and to see for themselves its beauty.

It is a well-known truism that when one must work for a goal, its attainment is better appreciated. During the summer scores of young people were selected to go to the site and there to take part in a work program. Scheduled for immediate construction were a combination meeting room-dining hall; several tent-type structures for temporary camper housing; a campsite for visitors who would bring their own housing facilities; a sauna; a waterfront; a dock; a complete water system; recreational facilities, and scores of lesser projects. It was an ambitious undertaking to erect a complete church camp in the wilderness. Only the faith that had made Central great could take to successful completion so extensive a construction program.

When the charter for the camp was granted, the objective stated was "to give emphasis to the Christian way of life through camping." Already this goal was being realized. All summer long the ambitious and the curious came to visit, some to stay to help for several days or a week, some to shake their heads in wonderment that such a vast project should be undertaken in so isolated a place. However, the work progressed; structures grew where only trees had thrived before, and fields were created out of woodlands. Before the summer ended, doubts no longer existed. Amnicon was a success.

"Our prayers have been answered," observed a member of the Board of Trustees that autumn.

"Right!" added a husky young teen-ager, as he surveyed his calloused hands. "But if we hadn't spent a

147

lot more time *working* than we did *praying*, I don't think these buildings would be here today."

Dr. Oliver Peterson, chairman of the Amnicon Board of Directors, reports:

"For two seasons now the youth of Central Lutheran Church have been brought together with urban youth of Minneapolis from several social agencies, inner-city schools and parishes. This setting provides person-to-person encounters and in-depth relationships so that the youth are better able to understand their reactions to others, to themselves, and to God. In short, they learn to live with one another in a Christian context. Christian community leaders are developed. Youth are shown the gratifications of service to others.

"In 1968, Camp Amnicon served over 350 campers. Camperships, given largely by members of Central Lutheran Church, enabled 176 inner-city youths to attend camp. Of this group, two thirds had never been to a camp before, and one third had never been out of the city before. The inner-city youth found that others care for them, and formed worthwhile impressions from the Christian leadership of the camp staff."

Dr. Morris Wee has commented on this remarkable youth activity: "A notable project is the use of Camp Amnicon to minister to the needs of the dispossessed youngsters of the inner city. Central's superb high school boys and girls took care of 170 of the neighborhood children at the camp last summer. Each child was financed by members of Central Lutheran church who gave a campership of $30 for each child. It was a unique, worthy and very remarkable ministry. Camp Amnicon has been a valuable tool in Central's hands for a modern, new-style ministry. We are most fortunate to have this camp for our use."

The gift of land on Lake Superior led to another acquisition of a larger tract on Minnesota's Lake of the Woods a year later. Living in Poplar, Wisconsin, were Mr. and Mrs. Robert Lundberg, ALC members. Mr. Lundberg owned several hardware stores in the area. Both of them became involved in the Amnicon River camp project, giving freely of their time and talents, he assisting in the construction of the first building on the site, and she as advisor to the girls' counselors. Together they owned 144 acres of land with a half mile of shoreline on Minnesota's largest lake, the Lake of the Woods. The property was rough and wild, with ridges of pink granite dividing it into natural valleys. The name of Chapel Rock was given to it by Milo Mickelson, former business administrator of Central, who visited the site.

"The property is so majestic that no matter where one stands it seems as if he is in a mighty chapel," said Mr. Mickelson.

This gift was turned over to the Amnicon board of directors, according to the wishes of the donors. According to present plans, this area is to be developed into a summer camp for the adult members of Central Lutheran Church.

Surely great progress had been made in the total program of Central Lutheran Church during the first five years of Dr. Wee's pastorate. But it was merely a preview of "service to others" that was to extend itself into the future.

CHAPTER **12**

A New Era
of Spiritual Vitality

"Commitment — Now!"

In 1969 the church stood on the threshold of another
half century of progress in its onward march to serve its
members, its God and its community. When we asked
Dr. Wee to summarize the accomplishments of Central
Lutheran Church during his ministry, he responded
with this statement:

"It has been a time of moving steadily forward in a
period of sudden and revolutionary changes in our city,
society and nation. The area in which the church is
located has been depopulated and has undergone
enormous change. The problems of the disinherited
people and of the war in Vietnam have been disquieting
to everybody. In this sociological upheaval, Central
Lutheran Church has gone about its task of serving the
people of Minneapolis and the Midwest in the name of
Jesus Christ.

"Internally we have seen the strengthening of some of
the structures to enable Central to move effectively in
meeting the changing situations and the emerging
challenges. This is reflected in the following:

• A dramatically new concept of an inner-city ministry
  through the establishment of Camp Amnicon.

- A new and vigorous youth committee with special attention on high school youth.

- A new board of parish education with an upgrading of church school curriculum.

- A new board of social justice to help Central cope with the civil rights crises.

- A broad and comprehensive ministry to the sick and the shut-ins through the Friendly Visitors.

- A strong and relevant Sunday evening program beamed mainly at the young adults.

"The new sensitivity to the inner-city needs is suggested by a strengthening of the Life and Growth program. The tutorial program for the slow learners in the neighborhood schools, a generosity in terms of concern, time and money on the part of Central's members in serving the needs of the dispossesed and a new format for special services focusing upon the minority population.

"Externally there has been the acquisition of more land for parking, the expansion of the radio ministry to include WCAL as well as KSTP, and the enlargement of the pastoral staff to include a youth pastor and a pastor for parish education. A study has been undertaken to identify the future development of the congregation in relation to the prospective expansion of the city of Minneapolis and the increasing awareness of the need for church-sponsored adult education.

"The stewardship program has remained healthy, membership pledges increased from $283,000 in 1962 to $370,000 in 1968. In this period, membership and church attendance have held slightly more than their own, while attendance at Holy Communion has advanced markedly.

The strength of the congregation as reflected in the statistics is notable chiefly because it is in sharp contrast to the declines of inner-city congregations in Minneapolis and elsewhere."

An important decision was made by the Board of Trustees in 1966 to secure the services of the American City Bureau of Chicago to make a survey of the potential growth and expansion of the physical facilities of Central Lutheran Church. Dr. Orville Dahl was assigned to make the survey. Out of it developed the concept of Central City.

Eight months of analyses were made of Central Lutheran Church, its activities, its programs, and its personnel, as well as the need for continuing land acquisition. Consultations were held with settlement houses, welfare agencies, civic leaders and officials involved in urban planning, and many others. Out of the comprehensive study, Dr. Dahl made several recommendations:

"The flight to the suburbs, blighted inner cities, lack of space, substandard residential areas, traffic congestion, limited recreational areas, all are symptomatic of the larger problem of modern urbanization. In larger part it is the problem of orienting the church to urban life that stimulates the idea of an assemblage of services for adults of all ages in the form of Central City.

"As Central Lutheran Church looks out upon its community filled with teeming thousands of human beings, what kind of individuals does it see? Most often it sees the adult, ranging from boys and girls in the process of becoming young men and women to elderly ladies and gentlemen. This span of years can easily cover four, five, six, or even seven decades of life! The church also sees children — ranging from the first moments of life to the end of youth. No other institution in society attempts to reach all people at every age except the church. The wonder is not that the church may lack efficiency at some points in a program so vast, but that it dares to undertake it at all.

"The idea of 'Central City' — deriving its name from the church that sponsors the concept — can be described from two points of view:

"First, insofar as its program identifies its purpose, Central City is a broadened ministry to young adults, and all other adults. It is pointed out by members of the clerical staff that there are now more than 100,000 men and women in the 18 to 24-age bracket in the city of Minneapolis, and that the largest concentration of young adults is in the Loring Park district. Furthermore, it is estimated that in the past decade, 30 percent of these young adults migrated to Minneapolis from rural areas and towns in Minnesota and from neighboring states. It is predicted that there will be more than 148,000 young adults in the city by 1970.

"Central City is a concept of services and facilities, then, that will help reach out to this group and become the way in which a dialogue is established. Central City is, then, a center with lounges, program hall, seminar rooms, food services, and recreational facilities such as a bowling alley, swimming pool, and activity rooms. At the heart of the whole process is an educational program ranging across the gamut of interests of young people. In preliminary analyses, Central City has confined itself, to the largest extent, with the needs of young adults. In short, the first comprehensible view of Central City makes of it a quasi-institution for young adults not unlike the YMCA and YWCA.

"Second, insofar as Central City involves facilities, it is a scheme for the practical use of the land that Central Lutheran Church owns now and that which it hopes to acquire in the future. In this sense, Central City is a physical grouping of facilities, buildings, and services underscoring:

a. The need to enlarge the facilities now centered in the parish house.

b. The need to provide facilities for the educational and activity programs of Central City for young adults and others.

c. The need to determine the feasibility of sponsoring a housing project for senior citizens and others, including the young adults.

d. The need to define a set of policies governing the parking needs of the congregation.

"These two broad questions, then, are the main objectives of this study: First, 'What is Central City in terms of a program?' and second, 'What is Central City in terms of a physical development plan?'

The final recommendations of the American City Bureau incorporate the following proposals:

1. The proposed chapel be an integral part of the existing sanctuary and be enclosed with a cloister-garth to be designed as a part of a new main entrance to the parish house from 14th Street.

2. An enlargement of the sacristy.

3. That a bell tower be designed as a campanile to be located on the corner of Fourth Avenue South and Grant Street.

Convention of American Lutheran Church at Central

Sunday Morning Nursery

Processional of Lutheran World Assembly delegates from Central
to Municipal Auditorium

Members of the Altar Guild at work

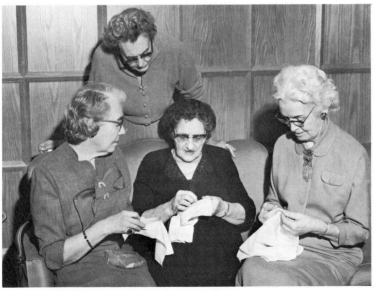

Altar Guild members sewing Baptismal napkins

Preparing for a wedding reception

Opening the campaign for "Greater Central"

View of the Altar, Lent 1961

Frederic Hilary, Minister of Music

Joyce Hilary at the Cassavant Organ

4. That a Central service building be designed for business administration, food services, housekeeping services and other facilities.

   5. That the congregation of Central Lutheran Church continue to develop a comprehensive program of adult education as a main part of its mission in Christian education for persons of post-high school age, a program of adult education for continuing education in all phases. This is to become known as a Center for Continuing Education.

6. A housing program for senior citizens if a need developed.

7. A development of increased parking facilities with a look to the future of building a parking ramp.

We cannot overlook the education program of the church since it is so essential to the training of the young. Christian education of its youth was one of the earliest concerns of Central's congregation. The Sunday School was one of the first organizations of the church, with a staff of three teachers and eleven pupils with Randolph Holland as the first superintendent. He was followed by O. J. Thorpe. In the fall of 1924, L. M. Brings became the general superintendent and served for fifteen years, succeeded by Lloyd Refsell. Mr. Glen Hoople became the general superintendent in 1945, which was the beginning of a long and efficient contribution to the Sunday School, continuing until his untimely death in December 1967. The next superintendent was Wayne Bengtson. Each successive year there has been a continued growth until the current enrollment of 750 pupils and a staff of 175 teachers and officers. The present superintendent is Myrt Kettner.

With the coming of Pastor Maynard B. Iverson in 1949 as Youth Pastor, a Junior Worship program was begun and held in "Old Central" preceding the instruction period. This was a complete worship service with junior ushers and a robed children's choir. This service did much to enrich and inspire the lives of the children and made meaningful the liturgy of the Lutheran Church.

Central Lutheran Church has always been sensitive to the needs of the neighborhood children and responded in 1961 by organizing two Saturday morning classes: a creative art class and a story hour. Also in 1961, a second session of the Sunday School was begun with a staff of twenty-five workers for the convenience of parents who are members of the Senior Choir.

The Sunday School was a year-round program for the children in the early years of the church's history. In 1929, a new dimension was added to the religious instruction — the daily Vacation Bible School which gave the equivalent of an entire year of Sunday School classwork. Children of kindergarten age up to fifteen years were enrolled that first summer. Over 120 pupils and teachers attended the three-week session. The variety of activities included Bible study, handicraft, motion pictures and lantern slides, and diamond ball games on the grounds of the Vocational School. That first Bible School was climaxed with a program in new Central and a picnic the last day in Loring Park.

This program has been continued up to the present. Creativity has always been encouraged in the children. Puppet shows, dramatizations, and a talking clown have charmed the children and illustrated the daily lessons. Worship through music has been stressed, and the homeward bound cars have reverberated with the joyous songs learned in Bible School.

In 1966, an enrollment record of 300 boys and girls was achieved. In 1967, two identical sessions were held in July and August so that more children could attend. The name was changed to Vacation Church School, but the goals have remained the same. In addition to furthering the Christian education of Central's own children, this important summertime program has contributed to the local mission work of the church. Class rolls include children from other churches and from unchurched families in the neighborhood.

In April 1965, Eleanor Schultz became the first director of the parish education program. During her two years of service, expanded programs with an improved curriculum, visual aids and additional teacher training classes were added.

But an enlargement of the program occurred in 1967 when the Rev. David L. Anderson became the second director of the Education Department. Now this department includes the Sunday Church School, direction of Confirmation classes, the Vacation Church School, Adult Education, and the Bethel Bible Study series. Betty Brekke is the present director of Education.

The following poem summarizes the thinking of the adults of Central Lutheran Church in supporting the education program, particularly as it relates to children:

THE BRIDGE-BUILDER

An old man going down a lone highway
Came at the evening, cold and gray,
To a chasm vast and wide and steep,
With waters rolling cold and deep.
The old man crossed in the twilight dim,

The sullen stream had no fears for him;
But he turned when safe on the other side,
And built a bridge to span the tide.
"Old man," said a fellow pilgrim near,
"You are wasting your strength with building here.
Your journey will end with the ending day,
You never again will pass this way.
You've crossed the chasm, deep and wide,
Why build you this bridge at eventide?"
The builder lifted his old gray head.
"Good friend, in the path I have come," he said,
"There followeth after me today
A youth whose feet must pass this way.
The chasm that was as naught to me
To that fair-haired youth may a pitfall be;
He, too, must cross in the twilight dim —
Good friend, I am building this bridge for him."
                              —Will Allen Dromgoole

We cannot overlook the impact of the Bethel Bible courses of instruction, originated by the Rev. Harland Swiggum and Dr. Wee at Bethel Church in Madison, upon the religious life of Central's members. After the two-year training period for the first teachers during 1961-62, over 400 were enrolled in the classes beginning in 1963, which was increased to 500 the next year, 750 in 1966, and over 900 in 1967. There will be a continuing interest in these courses until almost the entire congregation will have completed one or more courses of instruction. "The principle underlying this program in Central," says Pastor Thompson, "is simple. We must know God's Word if we are ever going to live it."

Central Lutheran Church has always carried on a program of serving minority groups at home and abroad, as is evidenced by the work of the members of the Martha Mission in supplying clothing for unfortunate people in Minneapolis and elsewhere. Likewise, there was a helping hand extended to the Latvians and American Indians over the years.

More recently this interest was extended to include participation in Project Summer Hope when special meetings were held and various ethnic speakers explained their problems. A course of instruction was offered to members during the summer months.

The American Lutheran Church had requested its 5,000 congregations to support the human rights program, and "Central's participation in it was most excellent. Among the results of the project were the following: a new understanding of the black community, a new insight concerning white racism, a developing sense of personal and corporate responsibility on human justice and the establishment of Central Lutheran Church as a church of human justice . . ." so reported Dr. Wee at the 1969 annual meeting. This project is another example of Central's participation in meeting certain problems of the community head on. The church has always become involved in worthwhile causes, such as public education, the United Fund, the Red Cross, and other charitable projects.

Recognizing Central's active program in this area, Governor Harold LeVander appointed Dr. Wee, in 1967, to become the chairman of a fifteen-member State Board of Human Rights. The church itself will continue its support of the problem. A Board of Social Justice has been activated to keep the congregation aware of its responsibilities to solve these community problems.

For over three years a Golden Anniversary Committee under the chairmanship of P. Don Carson met frequently to make plans for the 50th anniversary observance. A search was made for a theme. It was selected in late 1968. The Life and Growth Committee had recommended that members read the book, "Fire in Coventry," which is the story of the rebuilding and dedication of the bombed-out cathedral at Coventry, England. In the program of rebuilding the cathedral, there arose the idea that there should be a rededication of the members of the cathedral. The story of how this spirit-filled movement gripped the people is exciting. "Could this same experience of renewal and rededication of our people be a slogan for Central's 50th anniversary?"

At a special committee meeting the idea was discussed. A theme emerged for the anniversary year: "Commitment — Now." It was decided that every member be urged to purchase a copy of "Fire in Coventry," and that a program of renewal and rededication be started at Central. Immediately a thousand copies of the book were placed on sale in the bookstore.

The immediate result was a decision to devote the entire year of 1969 to a program of rededication as a servant church in the community. All organizations of the church were to become involved. "Why not set aside a time for a series of special spiritual renewal meetings at the beginning of Lent?" The result was that Dr. Arndt Halvorson of Luther Theological Seminary conducted four special services. The new format and approach was carried on during the Lenten services, climaxing this spiritual renewal effort on Palm Sunday with the reception of a large class of new members.

"We think this emphasis of 'Commitment — Now' will justify the fifty years of history and launch our congregation into a new era of spiritual vitality, religious awareness and social dedication. It could be the most exciting and significant thing to happen in 1969," said Dr. Wee.

Special reunions of choirs, ushers, youth groups, confirmation classes and other organizations were held during 1969.

The highlight of the Jubilee Year was the appearance of the golden anniversary preachers in April: Dr. Frederick Schiotz, president of the American Lutheran Church, and two former pastors, Dr. Elmer S. Hjortland and Dr. A. Reuben Gornitzka, topped by the outstanding anniversary banquet held at the Leamington Hotel on May 2 with former Congressman Dr. Walter H. Judd as the speaker.

The results of this anniversary year will be two-fold: First, as Dr. Wee has said: "The anniversary should mark a new commitment of the congregation and of each member to Jesus Christ as Savior, God and Lord. The finest thank offering we could bring to the great God who has walked each day with this congregation would be the commitment and dedication of our lives to Christ and His holy purposes." Second, an influx of new members as a result of the efforts of present members to influence friends, relatives and the unchurched to join forces to continue the destiny of Central Lutheran Church as a servant church in the next half century."

CHAPTER 13

The Beautiful Cathedral Windows

"To represent our faith, and our love of freedom and truth"

As an explanation of, and a reason for, the use of the particular kind of windows and decorations which beautify and make impressive the sanctuary of Central, we quote from the designer of the windows:

"It is not our desire to describe the architectural beauty of Central Lutheran Church. We cannot but feel that here is a worthy casket built to hold securely the spiritual treasures within. Its wall resting on a foundation imbedded firmly in the earth, give us an impression of solidity and strength; its buttresses holding up the walls, symbolize courage and fortitude; the beautiful tracery of the windows shows us grace and lightness as they grow upwards like a vine, almost to the roof upon which is firmly planted Christ's own symbol, the cross. Approaching the entrance of the church we feel again the words of the Psalmist, 'Enter into His gates with thanksgiving; and into His courts with praise.' This impression holds us as we pass through the portals, for we feel we are within a House of God, designed and decorated with a beauty that is sanctified. The rich gold coloring of the walls, the jewelled splendor of the stained glass windows, the long center aisle — all seem to lead us directly to the chancel and tell us symbolically that Central Lutheran Church has been built as a magnificent setting for the Altar.

A writer has said of the windows in Central: "They are past all description — beautiful! They glow in all the colors of the rainbow. High and wide they permit a soft and pleasant light to flood the entire church." Again and again visitors have remarked on the glory of their color. Nevertheless, they are restful and help us to feel that we are in the house of God.

These twenty-five windows are made entirely of imported glass and are designed and painted in hard color, thus carrying out all the methods employed by the craftsman of the mediaeval period, and are as lasting as the windows now in place in the cathedrals of Europe. If measured in dollar value, these windows have been appraised at a present value of $800,000, and are no longer available in this type of glass.

Owing to the size of the four large windows — the transept and chancel windows are 22 feet by 35 feet — showing directly in the auditorium of the church, it was decided to dispense with figure work or symbolic representations of the Scriptures, and carry out the windows in Gothic Graisaille effects and thus give to these tall, slender openings a feeling of laciness, similiar in character to the famous windows of Westminster Cathedral. Likewise a similar design was followed on the sixteen large windows on the balcony level and the sixteen windows on the upper ceiling level.

This conception by Dr. Stub of the proper design and color scheme for the windows has proven correct, for the sparkling jewelled richness of color when brightened by the sun's rays, has been softened and subdued by the artists, so that the light shining into the auditorium of the church, preserves that feeling of peace and reverence only found in mediaeval glass.

Color symbolism in glass usually follows these thoughts:

White stands for innocence and joy.

Red — the fire of love which the Holy Spirit kindles and sheds forth within us.

Green — the hope and desire of Heaven.

Purple — penitence and reminder of our Lord's passion.

Gold — glory, victory!

Blue — steadfastness, loyalty.

In the lower windows, showing on the side aisles of the auditorium, is carried out a concept of Dr. Stub's, showing the great countries which have embraced the faith of Luther since the Reformation, arranged in chronological order. These countries are represented by their national shield which is mounted by a crown, back of which is shown the cross of the Reformation.

The universal or ecumenical nature of the Reformation is symbolized by the emblems in the sixteen lancets, or panels, two in each of the eight windows on the first floor. In the center of each panel is a true quatrefoil containing the following:

The square cross, symbolic of the Reformation principles.

A crown, the symbol of victory, at the top of the cross.

A national emblem just beneath the crown. Each symbol represents a nation which has taken an important part in the extension of the Reformation principles.

One of the four windows in the corners of the balcony.

The window in the Baptismal Chapel.

The flag of Germany, the mother country of the Reformation. Paired with Germany is the Saxon lion on a field of gold, in memory of the greatest Saxon of them all — Dr. Martin Luther.

The blue and gold flag of the Kingdom of Sweden and the blue and white cross flag of Finland. Under God, it was Gustavus Adolphus, the hero of the Thirty Years' War, with his blue clad Swedes and Finns, who saved the day when Germany lay prostrate.

The flag of the Kingdom of Denmark, always a staunch supporter of Reformation principles, paired with the red, white and blue cross flag of the Kingdom of Norway, whose liberty-loving people never yielded entirely to the despotic sway of Medieval hierarchy.

The blue, white and red cross flag of Iceland, which has the oldest parliament in existence and gave to the western world their modern systems of government, together with the old flag of Russia. Before World War I about three million Russians were members of the Evangelical faith. No one suffered more for their faith than these brave and loyal people.

The flag of the Kingdom of Holland paired with the flag of Switzerland. The earliest American Lutherans came from Holland. John Calvin is typical of the uncompromising nature of the freedom-loving Swiss people.

The tri-color of France is placed in recognition of the brave Hugenots together with the broadbarred flag of old Britain (What heroes she has reared for the faith! What an influence the English Bible has wielded!).

The flag of Poland and the flag of old Scotland with its St. Andrew's cross. The Polish flag reminds us of the Bohemian, John Huss. Though Poland today is not a Protestant nation, so many of her sons and daughters have died and bled for the faith that they need to be remembered. And what an influence Scotland has had with its church leaders, poets and princes among preachers.

The beautiful Star Spangled Banner is placed at the right of the chancel — the Gospel side, therefore the place of honor. The flag of the Dominion of Canada is its companion.

This is one of the four Transept and chancel
windows.

The twenty-five stained glass windows have an appraised replacement value of $800,000. But the precious type of glass cannot be furnished now.

These emblems are a representation of our faith, our love of freedom and truth, and our parliamentary systems of government. We give God the glory for what our forebears did to preserve for us the old Gospel truths.

CHAPTER **14**

Central Lutheran
Church Today

*"The present is the past rolled up for action, and the past is
the present unrolled for understanding."*
— Will and Ariel Durant

On Sunday afternoon, September fifteenth, 1971, the church celebrated Dr. Morris Wee's 40th anniversary. At this service Dr. Wee made the startling announcement that he was retiring from the ministry at the end of the year. A call committee was elected immediately to fill the vacancy with Merlin Hovden as chairman. Several candidates were proposed but the final choice was Hoover T. Grimsby who had a track record of twenty-seven years in the ministry, two years in Austin, Minnesota, and twenty-five years in Milwaukee, Wisconsin.

God's will works in mysterious ways for it seemed to be ordained that a call was to be sent to someone who grew up in Central Lutheran Church. It was in 1930 that Rev. Henry P. Grimsby with his wife and son Hoover came to Central from Bethel Lutheran Church in Minneapolis where he had been the pastor for twenty-five years, and in 1930 became chaplain of the Lutheran Welfare Society of Minnesota. The family was immediately accepted at Central, and Hoover was conscripted by Supt. Lawrence Brings to play the organ and sometimes the piano for the opening worship in the high school department in the sanctuary. He assumed this responsibility for ten years.

This became his Sunday schedule while attending Roosevelt High School, the University of Minnesota, and Luther Theological Seminary. His school graduation was held at Central, at which time he played "Toccata in C Major" by Bach as a part of the program. Young Hoover later attended the University of Chicago and studied organ under Mr. Mack Evans and Dr. Frederic Marryott. If he hadn't enrolled at the University of Minnesota he might have become our organist instead of our senior pastor.

His ordination service took place in Central Lutheran in January, 1945. He left Central to accept a call to Ascension Lutheran Church in Milwaukee as associate pastor, and after five years he became the senior pastor, a position he held until 1970.

It must have been the Holy Spirit that called Pastor Grimsby to come back home to Central after an absence of 27 years. The determining factor which made the difference in accepting the call was the strong spiritual-directed leadership of the church, and the vital participation of the members in worship, and in all the varied projects of the community as is exemplified by its motto as a servant church. Central is located in the very heart of the city, and her heart must beat daily with the love of Christ for all people. The varied backgrounds of the members of the church provided a marvelous opportunity for a future ministry, and Dr. Grimsby wanted to be a part of it.

While in Milwaukee Dr. Grimsby was privileged to serve on many boards, committees and commissions, both in church and community ventures. He has been a member of the Board of Trustees of Carthage College since 1970 and Golden Valley Lutheran College since 1971.

Hoover Grimsby assumed his position as senior pastor of Central Lutheran Church on September 1, 1972 and preached his first sermon on September 10. He was installed on September 24 by Dr. J. Elmo Agrimson, Bishop of the Southeastern Minnesota District. He immediately entered into his responsibilities by adding staff members — Pastors Timothy Hepner, George Weinman and Jonas O. Jovaag.

The high point of the entire year was "Celebration Night" when the three former senior pastors returned to celebrate with the members the burning of the parish house mortgage. The entire evening emphasized gratitude, fellowship, and commitment to the life and programs of Central. It was an occasion when the members were fired with a new enthusiasm, new dreams, and new services for the future.

In this historical narrative it is impossible to record all the daily activities of organizations, individuals and staff members or to relate the intimate impact on people by the various services of the church. It becomes necessary, therefore, to emphasize the highlights as they relate to the basic program of the church.

On Sunday afternoon, November 18, 1973, a reception was held to honor Fred and Joyce Hilary for 20 years of service as Director of Music and Church Organist. Under the Hilarys' devoted and capable leadership, Central's choirs have gained a national reputation for excellence. The list of their service and accomplishments since they came in 1953 is outstanding — twenty-three continuous presentations of "Christmas at Central"; five senior choir performances with the Minnesota Orchestra at Northrup Auditorium; senior choir appearance on several CBS and NBC national and international broadcasts; the telestar broadcast from Bethlehem in Israel at Christmas 1972, and 20 outstanding oratorios in observance of Central's Palm Sunday Anniversary date and 10 years planning and organizing the organ symposium which has developed into the largest in the country.

The Evangels of Central Lutheran were formed in 1974. They describe themselves as a group of individuals who have tasted the sweetness of God's love and found God's rich supply of grace and are spreading the glad tidings to others. The purpose of the Evangels is to share God's love by demonstrating that members of Central Lutheran Church care about all God's children. They will show Christian concern for and welcome into Central's midst all visitors at Central. New people moving into the community, friends and neighbors, business acquaintances, people seeking information about Central as well as anyone else with whom they may come in contact. The Evangels are a group of Central Lutheran Church members who are growing in their Christian faith and who wish to experience this growth in action and commitment and outreach.

During the spring of 1975 a United Mission Appeal was launched which succeeded in raising pledges of over $400,000 to be paid over a three-year period. The church's obligation to the ALC and the Lutheran Social Service was met and over $200,000 was paid on the church's indebtedness.

In 1975 the Friendly Visitors celebrated ten years of visitation, 230 members had been involved in visiting shut-ins and the elderly on a one-to-one basis. Since its inception 405 visitors and 539 shut-ins have been involved with a total of 27,038 personal visits. This service is continued under the leadership of Helen Rusten and Agnes Hoople.

The Clothes Closet and Food Pantry continue to minister to hundreds of disadvantaged people in the community. About 50 women of Central are involved in the distribution of this material on Monday mornings. The distribution of clothing is growing with the involvement of more individuals and groups around the state. The congregation has provided more than 175 families with food and toys at Christmas time.

The Center for Children continues to serve elementary and junior high children of the neighborhood. The congregation provides the building and utilities to keep neighborhood children off the streets and usually out of trouble, and the staff and several volunteers lead a program teaching self-respect and a sense of responsibility through recreational, educational and social activities. Aside from the annual budget of $4,000 by the congregation, neighboring churches, foundations and corporations give financial aid to carry on this worthwhile program.

The 60th anniversary of Central was observed on September 5, 1979, when the three former senior pastors, Dr. Wee, Dr. Gornitzka and Dr. Hjortland gave the keynote addresses when a Renewal Program for structural improvements to the buildings was announced after a previous decision of the congregation made in February 1979. The slogan adopted for a campaign to raise at least $520,900 is "Rejoice in the Past — Improve for the Future."

Another outstanding event occurred on May 16, 1976 when the senior choir presented Brahms' "Requiem" in the Minneapolis Orchestra Hall. This was indeed a musical adventure, and a sterling presentation, which was superb, given by the choir and the orchestra. It was a significant event in the life of Frederic Hilary, the director, because his mother was a soprano soloist when Brahms directed the Requiem himself in the city of Dresden, Germany.

In the summer of 1978 Fred and Joyce Hilary completed 24 years of devoted service to Central and its music program. A recognition of their unselfish years of developing a high standard of church music was observed at a Sunday afternoon meeting in June to show appreciation of their accomplishment in expanding the church's music program.

"To inherit this great tradition of music, and capitalize on it, requires the best in ability and commitment." A Search Committee devoted six months to interview prospects to succeed the departing Hilarys. Dr. John A. Ferguson was recommended unanimously and he accepted the call to become director of music and as organist. He is eminently qualified for this position. He received a doctor's degree from the Eastman School of Music and has served on the music faculty of Kent State University since 1963 until he joined us at Central in September, 1978.

Dr. Ferguson has established a fine reputation as a concert artist and clinician with many appearances each season throughout the country. He was organist/ choirmaster at Kent United Church of Christ. He was a member of the hymnal committee and served as music editor for the new United Church of Christ hymnal published in 1974. At Central Dr. Ferguson has already demonstrated the wisdom of his selection and has won the acceptance by choir members for his able musicianship.

CHAPTER 15

A Giant Step Forward

"I find the great thing in this world is not so much where we stand, as in what direction we are moving."
— Oliver Wendell Holmes

In preparation for the celebration of the sixtieth anniversary of the church, considerable discussion and planning continued from 1976 for three years by the staff and lay leaders. It was realized that a changing world with new problems had forced a re-assessment of our new obligations and responsibilities if we were to fulfill our destiny as a servant church to our members, to the community and to the world.

As the new organizational structure was being evolved, it arose out of our basic confession that:

"Central Lutheran Church was established in 1919 to provide a base for a ministry to meet the needs of the neighborhood, the metropolitan community and the world.

"We are a people created and chosen by God; redeemed, reconciled, and forgiven by the life, death, and resurrection of Jesus Christ; and empowered by the Holy Spirit to serve one another.

"At the center of our life together is a preaching and teaching ministry that equips persons in their own uniqueness to: witness to their faith, pray with their lives, and serve without thought of return. We are a worshipping community which comes together to give strength to one another and to share the collective resources we possess for the building of God's Kingdom.

"Reaching out in faith and love, we reaffirm our commitment to follow the Gospel in a global context."

To accomplish this expanded mission of Central Lutheran Church in a changing world, a "Design of Ministry" was developed and accepted for adoption by the congregation. To authorize this new plan, it was necessary to amend and restate the Articles of Incorporation of Central Lutheran Church, which was approved and passed by the congregation on Nov. 21, 1978.

To foster a greater participation of members in the active day-by-day life of the church, it established ten centers of a ministry, involving a hundred participants, led by elected boards. Each board, in turn, is represented by a coordinating Council of Ministries with its chairperson. Other members of the Council of Ministries are the four elected officers of the congregation, and the senior pastor.

The ten boards are listed under three categories as follows: NURTURE: worship, care of persons, Christian education, youth; OUTREACH: evangelism, social ministry; MISSION SUPPORT: membership, stewardship, communications, trustees. The ministry of each board is carefully described in the by-laws to provide specific direction from the congregation to each board. The function of each board is to assure that its specific ministry is carried out through members of the congregation. The functions of the Council of Ministries are to coordinate the work of the boards, conduct long-range planning, and act for the congregation between congregational meetings. The duties of each board are outlined in detail, encompassing the usual types of activities associated with the goals mentioned below:

The Board of Worship is established to enable, encourage, and provide for the coming together of the congregation and the public community to: worship God the Father, the Lord Jesus Christ and the Holy Spirit; hear the Word of God; receive the sacraments of Baptism and Holy Communion; be renewed in faith and strength and peace; give strength to one another; and to share the diverse resources we possess for the building of God's Kingdom.

The Board for the Care of Persons is established to: nuture the spiritual welfare of the congregation, individually and corporately, and to equip the saints for the work of ministry, for building up the body of Christ.

The Board of Christian Education is established to: provide religious instruction for all age groups, and to plan a program that will strengthen the family as a basic unit of Christian education.

The Board of Youth is established to minister to youth and provide opportunities for the ministry of youth.

The Board of Evangelism is established to implement obedience to Christ's commission: "Go ye therefore and make disciples of all nations": by enlisting all of God's people in the work of bringing the Gospel of Jesus Christ to all people, members and others, whatever their situation or need; offering everyone the simple factual promise of a saved relationship with Jesus Christ; providing fellowship, teaching, sharing, and caring, in cooperation with appropriate boards, for all who are reached so as to continually increase the faith in and the knowledge of Jesus Christ within the fellowship.

The Board of Social Ministry is established to act out God's love by helping meet the needs of all people in relation to the social setting and the systems and institutions of human society.

The Board of Membership is established to bring to the family of God through the family of Central Lutheran Church all those who are seeking or need more opportunity to worship and serve in God's Kingdom.

The Board of Stewardship is established for: the achievement of good stewardship attitudes in members of the congregation; the training and commissioning of members of the congregation for the work of Christ's Kingdom; the development and implementation of a program of dedicated, proportionate, first-fruits giving.

The Board of Communications is established to: boldly proclaim the Gospel to both the congregation and the community; present to the community a Christian image reflecting the work of Christ; provide means for communication within the congregation; communicate the activities of the congregation to the community.

The Board of Trustees is established to manage the physical properties and financial assets of the congregation as a means of supporting the ministries of the congregation.

Dr. Grimsby in his report to the congregation in June, 1979, stated the objectives of the Ministry Design:

"The new structure has now been put into action, as a result of the congregational action in February. We have incorporated 100 people in the decision-making process of the church's life. This is a giant step forward. It has been absolutely thrilling to catch the initiative and vitality of the board members. Each board focuses its attention on a single area of our ministry, but appreciates the fact that there is a necessary overlap. The Council of Ministries, made up of the officers of the church, and the chairperson of each board, operates as a clearing house, and also gives the various heads of the boards an opportunity to work out ways and means of handling matters which have a natural overlap. I would say that we are off to a very good beginning.

"The commanding word of the officers, boards and committees as they work together in celebrating the Gospel during this special 60th year, is to emphasize the word IMPROVE. We must improve for the future. This involves spiritual renewal in all its facets, resulting in spiritual life and growth."

As we enter another decade of service, it will be inspirational to survey where we started from and how we reached our sixtieth year of accomplishment. The highlights are given below:

Jan. 3, 1919   Committee met to organize an English-speaking Lutheran church in downtown Minneapolis.

Feb. 28, 1919   Ten men incorporated Central Lutheran Church; 12 families became the first members.

Mar. 4, 1919   Dr. J. A. O. Stub accepted call to Central Lutheran Church.

Apr. 13, 1919   First services conducted on Palm Sunday. Dr. Stub installed as pastor.

Feb. 27, 1920	"Old Central," constructed in 1883 was purchased for $33,000. Membership — 220 families, 581 souls.
July 18, 1926	Ground broken for building of New Central.
Nov. 28, 1926	Cornerstone laid for New Central.
Dec. 25, 1927	First services in New Central conducted
Apr. 1, 1928	New Central dedicated on Palm Sunday. Cost of building — $576,469.
Dec. 31, 1939	Membership at end of first 20 years — 2,735 souls.
Aug. 7, 1940	Financial reorganization completed.
Oct. 23, 1942	Central Lutheran Church Endowment Fund established.
June 11, 1944	Dr. J. A. O. Stub passed away.
June 18, 1944	Dr. J. A. O. Stub Memorial Fund established in the Endowment Fund.
Aug. 19, 1945	Dr. E. S. Hjortland installed as senior pastor.
May 10, 1949	Thirtieth anniversary celebrated.
Dec. 31, 1949	Membership — 4,142 souls.
Jan. 1, 1950	Administration of business affairs reorganized with appointment of a business manager and executive secretary.
Nov. 19, 1950	First annual Every Member Canvass conducted. Pledged — $138,480.
Dec. 30, 1951	Ground broken for first unit of the parish house.
Feb. 20, 1952	Central Lutheran Foundation incorporated for purpose of managing the Endowment Funds of Central Lutheran Church.
May 25, 1952	Cornerstone laid for the first unit of the parish house.

Oct. 26, 1952	First unit of parish house dedicated. Cost of building — $242,258.
Dec. 31, 1954	Membership — 5,214 souls.
Oct. 15, 1955	Dr. E. S. Hjortland resigned as senior pastor.
Feb. 12, 1956	Dr. A. Reuben Gornitzka installed as senior pastor.
June 25, 1956	Demolition of "Old Central" stated.
Mar. 10, 1957	Cornerstone laid for second unit of parish house.
Aug. 4, 1957	Parish House dedicated. Cost of building — $628,187.
Aug. 15, 1957	Lutheran World Federation Third Assembly held with Central as host church. Closing rally held on Aug. 25
Aug. 1, 1958	Life and Growth program initiated.
Nov. 22, 1957	Church Library and Book Store opened; Ellen Ulland, Librarian.
Nov. 9, 1958	Ninth annual Every Member Canvass conducted. Pledged — $237,335.
Dec. 31, 1958	Membership — 5,393 souls.
Mar. 22, 1959	40th anniversary of first service conducted at Central Lutheran Church.
1962-1965	Congregation volunteered space to city-wide director of American Indian programs.
Easter, 1963	Dr. A. Reuben Gornitzka gives farewell sermon upon resignation as senior pastor.
Fall, 1963	Permanent Children's Library set up.
Oct. 13, 1963	Dr. Morris Wee installed as senior pastor.
Apr. 19, 1964	Dedication of Cassavant organ in sanctuary.

Oct. 18, 1964	45th anniversary of Central Lutheran Church's founding celebrated.
Nov. 1964	Congregation adopts theme "Central Lutheran — A Servant Church."
April, 1965	Eleanor Schultz named first Parish Education Director.
May 16, 1965	Organ and Choir festival in honor of 90th birthday of Dr. Albert Schweitzer. Performance of the "Messiah" by Senior Choir and Minneapolis Symphony musicians.
1965	Friendly Visitors program begun. In 1978, 211 homebound and elderly visited.
June 1, 1966	Leif R. Larson resigns after 16 years as first business administrator.
1966-1967	Congregation "loans" Dr. Morris Wee to direct the $20,000,000 fund-raising project for the American Lutheran Church colleges. The Rev. J. N. Quello temporarily serves as associate pastor during his absence.
Mar. 23, 1967	Articles of Incorporation drawn up for Camp Amnicon Foundation, providing Christian camping facilities on Lake Superior.
1968	Clothes Closet and Pantry are organized to aid needy persons.
1969	Year-long observance of 50th Golden Anniversary under the theme "Commitment — Now," highlighted by anniversary banquet on May 2.
1969	Publication of "What God Hath Wrought", a history of Central

	Lutheran congregation, written by Dr. Lawrence M. Brings.
Dec. 1971	Dr. Morris Wee retires as senior pastor.
1972	First annual "Ministry in Social Change" program undertaken in conjunction with Luther Theological Seminary.
1972	Support begins for missionaries Olav and Eunice Torvik in Madagascar.
Sept. 24, 1972	The Rev. Hoover T. Grimsby installed as senior pastor; still serving today.
Dec. 1972	Senior Choir tours Holy Land; broadcasts via telestar from Bethlehem on Christmas Eve.
Fall 1972	Center for Children, an after school and evening child development program for neighborhood children, is organized and housed in former NSP facility.
Sept. 21, 1973	"Spirit of Central" is changed from a monthly to a weekly church newsletter.
Nov. 16, 1973	First of annual "Spiritual Renewal" Events is held.
Jan. 6, 1974	Members vote to purchase David Agency property (now Central West).
Feb. 18, 1974	Downtown Montessori LaPepiniere School and Day Care Center opens in space provided by Central Lutheran Church.
July 7, 1974	Central Lutheran lay volunteers personally bring Holy Communion to shut-in members in their homes.
Aug. 1, 1974	Central welcomes and supports the Tran Family, refugees from Vietnam.

Oct. 19, 1974	Noel and Karen James commissioned to serve three years at a mission school in Eshowe, South Africa.
Nov. 3, 1974	King Olav V of Norway briefly visits Central Lutheran Church during his Twin Cities tour to observe the Sesquicentennial of Norwegian immigration.
Jan. 5, 1975	Worship II (contemporary, informal service) begins.
May 1, 1975	Congregation launches "Central Mission Appeal."
May 25, 1975	Senior Pastor Hoover T. Grimsby is conferred honorary degree of Doctor of Divinity by St. Olaf College.
July 1975	Judd Nelson beings self-supporting ministry at Chiayi Christian Hospital, Taiwan.
Nov. 13, 1975	"Grand Opening" of Leisure Time Center for senior citizens.
March 1976	Central officers and boards adopt a "Mission Statement" of purpose as guidelines for the congregation's ministry.
May 16, 1976	Senior Choir is first local church to sing in a concert at Orchestra Hall.
July 4, 1976	Central Luthern Church has festival worship in observance of the nation's Bicentennial.
July 16, 1976	Congregation begins major interior renovating of sanctuary; worships in a maze of scaffolding.
Aug. 1976	Congregation adopts the Kong Family, refugees from Laos.

Aug. 1977	Central's Business Administrator Clayton G. Spranger receives award as national Church Business Administrator of the Year.
Oct. 30, 1977	King Goodwill Zwelithini, king of the Zulu nation, worships and visits Central Lutheran Church during his nation-wide tour.
Apr. 16, 1978	Central officers and boards commission "Mission and Ministry" Committee to finalize Ministry Design document, for new organizational structure of the congregation.
Aug. 1, 1978	Frederic and Joyce Hilary retire after 24 years' service as music director and organist, respectively.
Sept. 1978	Dr. John Ferguson becomes organist and director of music.
Oct. 15, 1978	Bishop Josiah Kibira of Tanzania, president of the Lutheran World Federation, preaches at Central Lutheran Church.
Nov. 21, 1978	Congregation approves revised Articles of Incorporation, establishing a new form of organizational structure.
Dec. 3, 1978	Congregation officially uses new "Lutheran Book of Worship" for its services.
Feb. 27, 1979	Last Annual Meeting held under former organizational structure; complete roster of officers and boards elected to service under new structure.
Apr. 8, 1979	Congregation observes first of year-long celebration of 60th Anniversary.

| June 3, 1979 | Festival Celebration of Pentecost and Central's 60th Anniversary. |
| June 19, 1979 | First Annual Meeting under new organizational structure. |

Now as we enter our sixty-first year, we have assumed major projects and have widened our areas of service. Dedicated to our spiritual commitments, the membership adopted a budget of $1,000,000. for 1979-'80 at its June 19th annual meeting to underwrite the programs of the ten boards of the new Ministry structure. Thus, the membership proves its loyal support of a real spiritual thrust in the hearts and minds of people.

Cassavant Organ

Open Door Chapel, Camp Amnicon

The Cassavant Organ installed

Easter, 1965

Morning Worship Services at Central

A view of the Chancel and Altar

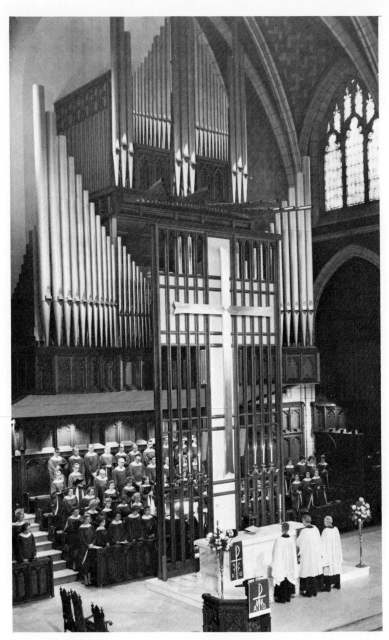

Worship Services

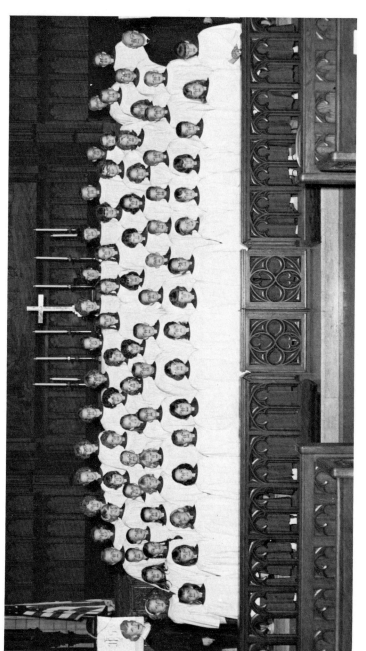

Carol Choir

Site of new recreation building overlooking Amnicon River

CHAPTER 16

The Stewardship of a Church's Finances

"Eyes that can see the dreams that good men dream."

Central Lutheran Church has a long record of service to others. It has consistently followed this ideal as the record will show. As each year of activity has unfolded over a half century, new challenges and new opportunities in a changing world appeared which required financial support by Central's members. They did not ignore the needs. They gave willingly and freely of their time and money to accomplish the church's destiny to become a servant church to the community.

That it was done with a grateful heart is evident in the long history of the church's policy of voluntary giving by its members. From the very beginning of the church in 1919, a practice was established. No pressure of any kind, direct or indirect, was to placed on any member to determine for him what his money contribution should be. To a large extent therein lies the financial success of Central Lutheran Church.

There never has been any listing of the pledges or contributions of individual members. Records of the annual contributions are kept inviolate in the files of the business office. No member, officer or pastor of the church has access to these cards. Only the business executive and his staff know the amount of an individual's giving. Even when a visitor calls on a member for his annual pledge, the card is inserted in a sealed envelope. The whole practice is premised on the experience that if a member has an awareness of the needs of the church, he will give according to his ability and dedication.

However, this policy does not mean that the laymen have shirked their responsibility to provide the financial means to support the program of the church. As early as December 1919, an every-member canvass was conducted and $11,500 in pledges for the year 1920 was secured. In December 1920, twenty teams of two each secured subscriptions of $18,800. From this time on an annual call was made on members to secure their pledges of support for the ensuing year.

In November 1957, a new idea was instituted to secure the annual pledges under the direction and supervision of Mr. Leif Larson. Five dinner meetings were held. The program of the church for 1958 was outlined by the pastors and the board chairmen. Pledges were made and it was found that half of the congregation had committed themselves. A committee of 500 members had volunteered to serve as visitors to call, two weeks later, on the remaining members who had not attended the dinners. On the basis of the total amount of pledges received, the budget for 1958 was determined. Incidentally, the Board of Trustees has always conducted the financial affairs so that expenditures do not exceed the budget allocations.

So successful was this first venture of holding dinners that the plan has continued as the annual method of securing pledges. The most fruitful by-product of the plan is that a group of 500 laymen have become dedicated in devoting their time in an important undertaking each year to guarantee the ongoing program of the church.

The following table provides interesting statistical information about the budget and membership during the past sixty years.

This table of statistics requires an explanation. As mentioned in a previous chapter, there has always been a shifting membership in Central Lutheran Church. As a downtown church, until recently, it attracted newcomers to the city who lived in the inner city. Many were students and young adults. Usually when marriage occurred, a home was purchased in the suburbs and a neighborhood church would be more convenient to attend. Separations were gladly made by Central. Thus, Central Church performed its missionary destiny by encouraging church membership, and after providing its service, passing its members on to suburban churches. However, it is likely that this situation in the next half century will revert to a more steady membership. No doubt the easy access to the church from all areas of the Twin Cities and suburbs because of the expanding interstate freeway systems will witness an increased membership in Central Church.

187

CENTRAL LUTHERAN CHURCH TOTAL INCOME — 1919-1978
(Exclusive of Endowment Fund)

Year	Budget	Income	Membership
1919	$ 7,000	$ 8,888.30	252
1920	11,500	17,330.23	581
1921	17,359	22,181.31	1031
1922	18,800	22,301.74	1348
1923	19,000	29,293.46	1548
1924	19,500	33,071.51	1548
1925	35,000	38,532.99	1852
1926	35,200	45,785.04	1900
1927	65,250	37,422.59	2117
1928	96,481	52,841.19	2222
1929	62,000	84,332.35	2170
1930	62,044	63,861.74	2209
1931	108,561	56,419.77	2355
1932	45,000	45,706.54	2432
1933	203,739	39,482.38	2561
1934	35,748	36,891.97	2802
1935	35,988	35,235.67	2700
1936	36,043	35,931.55	2539
1937	37,733	37,537.70	2577
1938	33,323	38,421.41	2622
1939	33,973	39,012.38	2611
1940	33,770	37,336.35	2735
1941	33,076	37,999.82	2728
1942	31,585	47,204.87	2746
1943	34,970	44,950.08	2633
1944	40,240	54,256.03	2600
1945	41,000	62,383.95	2686
1946	58,505	115,963.65*	2965
1947	76,650	161,054.34	3100
1948	92,115	141,024.48	3645
1949	100,525	146,291.24	3816
1950	109,385	182,956.54	4142
1951	122,530	224,431.34	4428
1952	127,445	256,642.25	4898
1953	138,620	258,428.74	4886
1954	152,220	278,492.40	4957
1955	169,320	283,045.14	5214
1956	173,620	324,325.58	5216
1957	213,120	350,211.13	5339
1958	308,000	372,478.79	5424
1959	328,700	369,868.22	5393
1960	355,700	402,373.00	5475
1961	394,500	436,620.00	5749
1962	400,150	449,593.00	5845
1963	431,000	516,036.00	5829
1964	454,900	516,861.00	5720
1965	475,000	539,399.00	5643
1966	504,500	546,445.00	5709
1967	537,650	576,990.00	5860
1968	653,320	636,100.00	5898
1969	628,420	615,200.00	5949
1970	622,510	621,321.00	6000
1971	629,030	673,248.00	6015
1972	640,200	660,334.00	5771+
1973	681,255	726,953.00	4234
1974	681,151	739,797.00	5181
1975	771,465	754,543.00	4869
1976	883,941	753,016.00	4820
1977	789,070	953,439.00	4767
1978	869,708	958,573.00	4762
1979	1,195,125		

+Policy started to eliminate inactive members.

*Includes LWA Offering — $10,443.00

The budget figures also require an interpretation since they do not reflect the total income of the church from year to year. For example, in 1924 the budget was $19,500, whereas the total income for the year was $33,071.51. Why? For many years one half of the seating capacity of 3,300 persons at worship services was occupied by visitors. The result was that plate offerings exceeded the pledged contributions of members. However, in the last fifteen years there has been a more realistic budget determination since the total income of the previous year was used as a basis of computation.

In order to carry on its service program, Central Lutheran Church has acquired land and facilities during the past sixty years. The condensed balance sheet as of December 31, 1978, listed assets of the church amounting to $3,534,215.68, and on a depreciated basis. If a replacement value of the sanctuary and parish house, plus parking lots, were to be appraised, it is estimated that the amount would be in excess of $8,000,000. Quite an accomplishment for a church that started out in 1919 with a membership of twelve families!

But we must not ignore the fact that members cannot conclude that their financial responsibility has ended The debt or liabilities as of December 31, 1978, amounted to $418,596.12. This sum is being paid off on a monthly amortization basis.

We cannot overlook the benevolence and mission program of Central Church that was inaugurated in 1919 when it was struggling to get started. This program has been continued without interruption through the years under the jurisdiction of the Board of Deacons. The report by this board of 1978 activities is indicative of every annual program in the past.

189

There were contributions of $427,446 to the mission and benevolence funds, and disbursements of $433,514. These funds were distributed as gifts to the American Lutheran Church synodical body and its departments, $86,276; Camp Amnicon, $15,400; the Greater Minneapolis Council of Churches, $1,023; and lesser amounts to Fairview Hospital, Ebenezer Home, Lutheran Deaconess Hospital, Radio Station WCAL, Plymouth Youth Center, American Bible Society, the Loring-Nicollet Council, United Church Women, New Hope Center, Lutheran Student Foundation, Holden Village, Lutheran Orient Mission, Gideons of Minneapolis, Golden Valley Lutheran College, Indian Mission, Minnesota Council of Churches, Scout Chaplaincy, Augustana Academy, Glen Lake County Home School, and others. In addition, the church supports Rev. and Mrs. Olav Torvick as Central's missionary family in Madagascar, Judd Nelson in Taiwan at his own expense, and Mr. and Mrs. Noel James in South Africa and at their own expense also.

In addition, the Board of Deacons disbursed in 1978, $323,223, for these activities: Parish Welfare Work; for parish education, including the Sunday School, Vacation Bible School, Confirmation classes, adult education, nursery, Sunday Evening at Central, and Life and Growth; Youth Work; the radio ministry; memorials; books and literature for the library; the art lending library; the Friendly Visitors.

To reveal the comprehensive opportunities for members at Central we need merely to refer to the 1968 Deacons' appeal: "If you want to be a guiding force in your church, join with other dedicated people who teach and work in the Sunday School, Daily Vacation Bible

School, work as nursery attendants, ushers, food service volunteers, office receptionists, Altar Guild ladies, Library and Book Nook attendants, the Floral Guild, Fine Arts, Parish Education, youth and adult programs, music and many others. There is a way for your talents to be used." There are numerous opportunities, therefore, for members to participate in activities of their own selection.

One of the main bulwarks for the financial security of Central Lutheran Church has been the establishment of the Central Lutheran Church Foundation.

An endowment fund was created in 1942 as a result of a bequest of $1,000 given to the church in the will of N.L. Enger. The next year two duplexes were given to the fund by Mr. F. A. Anderson. These gifts initiated a program of giving by various members to the endowment fund. Later it was considered advisable to protect the inviolability of the funds by organizing a separate corporate entity.

An outstanding example of laymen's initiative and responsibility was evidenced in 1944 when a decision was made by the Board of Trustees to conduct a special Silver Anniversary campaign to raise funds for the church's newly established endowment fund. A group of members under the co-chairmanship of A. R. Hustad and L. M. Brings made an appeal to Central's members and collected $25,000 in cash which was deposited in the fund. It must be realized that this occurred during the period when there was no senior pastor in charge to give counsel and direction.

In the winter of 1952, the Central Lutheran Church Foundation was incorporated under the laws of

Minnesota for the purpose of advancing the welfare, the growth and the ministry of Central Lutheran Church. A Board of Trustees consisting of twelve qualified members, was elected at the annual meeting of the congregation in January 1951, to administer the Foundation and to serve on the Board for life or for so long as they remained members of the church. The assets of the endowment fund, started in 1942, were turned over to the Foundation in 1955 by action of the congregation. Thereafter, the congregation would have no jurisdiction over the operation of the Foundation.

The Central Lutheran Church Foundation grew out of the need for a solid financial base to give stability to a congregation that had suffered real privation during the depression years. It became obvious that building an endowment fund, from which earnings could be used, offered a solution should economic stress and strain occur again.

There are many worthwhile causes in the Christian Church that need undergirding. The particular purpose of the Foundation is to strengthen the role of Central Lutheran as a "Servant Church" located in a busy downtown metropolitan area, reaching out in all directions to serve God and man.

Gifts to the Foundation made without specific designation as to the use of the earnings are the most desirable and helpful to the church in carrying out its program and ministry. However, every donor may exercise the privilege of restriction. Provision should then be made for use of the earnings in other ways if changed conditions no longer warrant the use of the earnings to the restricted purpose.

The reader may ask: How are gifts made to the Foundation? It can be done by memorial gifts, given in lieu of flowers. This is an enduring method to perpetuate the memory of one you hold dear, such as a relative, a devoted pastor, a faithful employer or employee, or a close friend. A memorial gift is a contribution of money, property or securities to a personalized memorial fund in the Foundation. Such gifts, along with similar memorial gifts, are held in perpetuity, with the earnings derived therefrom each year used for the welfare of Central Lutheran Church. Memorial gifts are often received annually in memory of loved ones who have passed on.

Of the various channels of capital gifts from individuals for church, charitable, and philanthropic purposes, the last will and testament is one of great importance. For the Christian, his lifetime plan of stewardship is not complete until he has made some provision in his will for the Lord's work and the extension of his Kingdom.

At present there are over 2150 individual family and memorial funds held in the Foundation. The income from the Foundation helps provide support of parish welfare work, educational programs, youth activities, building improvements, and other special needs, as determined by the donors and the Board of Trustees.

Gifts and bequests to the Foundation remain in perpetuity in the Foundation. Only the income from the principal, invested in mortgages and U.S. Government securities, is distributed annually to the church. Gifts may be made at any time by friends as well as members of the church. Memorial funds to departed loved ones predominate. There are, in addition, some direct contributions to the Foundation as individuals and families have seen the need for establishing perpetual income for the unique responsibilities of a downtown church.

With the resources that have been on hand, the Foundation secured control of the old debt on the sanctuary, which is now debt free. It also made loans to the congregation, which led to the construction of the parish house, purchases of parking lots, financing the chancel remodeling and securing the new Cassavant organ. This program of support is to be continued in the future.

The Foundation has consistently contributed its annual earnings to the church. During 27 years of its existence over a million dollars in earnings have been distributed to the Congregation.

The present members of the Board of Directors are: L. M. Brings, president; A. R. Hustad and Clifford C. Sommer, vice presidents; Jarl Olsen, secretary; L. R. Lunden, treasurer; B. N. Bell, F. W. Gaasedelen, James A. Halls, Elmer N. Olson, Dr. O. H. Peterson Jr., Dr. E. M. Rusten, and Glenn H. Steinke.

In a downtown church, many demands are made upon it beyond that of an ordinary congregation. Therefore, earnings from the Foundation help to care for needs that could otherwise not be satisfied. Moreover, control of the church indebtedness is also made possible by making loans from the Foundation to the church. Repayments are made to the Foundation on a monthly amortization basis out of special expansion funds pledged by the members each year. Thus it is unnecessary for the congregation to make outside loans to continue its program of building and land acquisition.

In the light of freeway and city auditorium developments, as well as those of Central Lutheran Church itself, it is anticipated that a two million-dollar endowment fund means added strength to the ministry of the church in what is most likely to become one of the most important geographical areas in Greater Minneapolis as well as the Upper Midwest. At the time of this writing, the Foundation assets exceeded $1,300,000.

In commenting about the value of the Foundation, Dr. Hoover Grimsby has stated:

"Central Lutheran has been called "the miracle church" — and rightly so. As a congregation it has thrived with the diversity and gifts of its members.

The miracle fund which has supported the program of Central Lutheran Church to such an amazing degree, is the Central Lutheran Church Foundation.

Over one million dollars in earnings has been passed on for programming to keep our miracle church vibrant and active in producing miracles in the form of care and concern among people living in the shadows of Central, as well as those living in the far reaches of our world.

All of us have been blessed to be a blessing by God's grace. Our Foundation becomes an instrument which is most valuable in extending God's Kingdom through Central Lutheran Church. It is our privilege to use the Foundation as an instrument to help us channel our gifts for present and future use in Kingdom service."

CHAPTER **17**

The March Into
The Future

"Lend me the stone strenght of the past,
And I will lend you the wings of the future."
— Robinson Jeffers

In the preceding chapters I have reviewed the accomplishments of the past in the life of a great church — sixty years of constant dedication to the ideal as a servant church. I have witnessed a continuing expanding program of basic services, both social and religious, to members and nonmembers alike during the first sixty years. So the past now becomes the prologue for the future. Central Lutheran should not retrench in its overall program. It must move forward to enlarge its service to its own members and the inner-city community, but on a much broader scale than ever before.

Each senior pastor during Central's first sixty years was a dedicated man who devoted his efforts in the advancement of Christ's Kingdom through our church, as revealed by statements they have made.

"The church must strive to be a real church home for people of all conditions and ages. It must 'teem with activity.' Its doors must be open in welcome to all, irrespective of antecedents or special position. It must be 'our Father's house,' where all can feel at home ... In other

196

words, the church does not exist so much for its members, as for what opportunity it gives them to serve our common Lord."

—*Dr. J. A. O. Stub*

* * * *

"Central Lutheran, because of its strategic location and its position of prominence in the Lutheran Church of America and in our synod, must always be a living, active, growing congregation. There is important work for all of us to do. We want our stewardship to be such that all churches shall be inspired by our faithfulness to Christ's program to 'make disciples of all nations.' "

—*Dr. Elmer S. Hjortland*

* * * *

"Centered then about the Gospel of a saving Christ, we dare to march on into tomorrow. By God's grace we do so as responsible Christians who each day are learning a bit better what it means to live within the 'communion of saints.' And learning this with gratitude, we seek above all else to win others into this same incomparable fellowship."

—*Dr. A. Reuben Gornitzka*

* * * *

"The next fifty years will doubtlessly be even more exciting and significant for Central than the past half century has been. We are living in the middle of an enormous revolutionary period — a time in which the witness to Christ's Gospel is essential to the life and existence of our world. But that Christian witness will need new forms in which to be expressed to a new world. The discovery of new ways to bring the old, old story of Jesus and His love will be the great adventure for us in the years ahead. God expects it of us — and we will not fail Him."

—*Dr. Morris Wee*

* * * *

"What a joyous privilege it is to serve as pastor of my 'home church.' Having attended Sunday School, having been confirmed and ordained at Central Lutheran Church places me in the very privileged position as being a son of the congregation. I find myself therefore, a debtor to the Sunday School teachers, the staff, and the many, many members of the congregation who gave me encouragement and direction during my formative years. I can only say *Gratias Deo* — thanks be to God. We are all debtors according to the Apostle Paul for grace upon grace, which has been bestowed upon us by Almighty God. We are thankful for the Word which has been preached and lived in our midst. The Sacraments have given us newness of life, which has allowed us to share our gifts with others, both at home and abroad. The first 60 years are but a prologue to the future. Let us now claim that future with renewed faith, and courageous action."

—Dr. Hoover T. Grimsby

It is at this point in the story that I must cease being an impersonal recorder of the events of the past. What I have written has been largely factual. Now I must become an oracle and forecast what I think is the destiny of the church in the future, however difficult it may be to anticipate the revolutionary changes that may occur from now until 2019. Of one fact I am certain: Central Lutheran Church must continue to expand its mission as a servant church. New heights of accomplishment must be reached, now even beyond our comprehension or vision. As we have done in the past, we must continue to adapt our program to the requirements of a changing world. For example, it is difficult for us to visualize what our approach will be in 2019. Only time will tell.

But what of the future? To be realistic, what will the next twenty-five years demand of us as a congregation? What are our challenges and our opportunities for service? I'll try to predict what I foresee as I dip into the future.

With a background of almost fifty-six years of membership in Central Lutheran Church and as an active participant during almost every year in some important activity of the church, I am aware of the problems, the heartaches, the difficulties and the achievements of the past. It is a springboard to help me judge the program and challenges for Central's greater service during the next twenty-five or fifty years.

Just as the twelve founders of Central had explicit objectives in 1919 when they organized the church, so we are now embarking on a twenty-five year plan to specifically accomplish our objectives. With a long-range plan before us for consideration and action, we can anticipate an ever-widening circle of influence of service to others.

The only justification for the existence of the Christian Church is that it makes possible the banding together of the followers of Jesus Christ, to live in accordance with His precepts, to help the poor, the sick and the needy, and to be guided by the Holy Spirit to follow in the footsteps of the Master. To share this experience with others requires dedication and enthusiasm.

I propose, therefore, that our primary objective should be a planned, concerted effort to increase the membership of the church — to set a goal of adding five hundred new members annually, in excess of separations. This should be an ongoing, continuous program supervised by the ten boards of Central. This is possible to achieve if each member of the congregation heeds the appeal to secure one new member annually.

To assist in achieving this goal, the pastoral staff should be organized so that annually each member will be visited in his home at least once, whether requested or not. These friendly visits would have far-reaching results in securing a close communication between members and the church.

The Pastor's Cabinet, originally created by Dr. Hjortland in 1946, and conducted for several years, was largely responsible for the rapid growth in membership. It should be revived again since it is effective in establishing a person-to-person relationship. Neighborhood groups of ten or twelve families with a member and his wife as co-chairpersons of each unit will result in closer relationships and will be effective to securing new members, establishing social and spiritual contacts, and assisting in supporting all the activities of the congregation.

To undergird this program it will be imperative that we establish a permanent public relations and publicity committee to relate the story of Central and its program; to keep the public informed of important activities of the church week by week. It would help to keep the name of Central before people by conducting a daily radio or TV program of inspiration, conducted by one or more of the pastors of Central.

I propose that the pastoral staff of Central be enlarged to adequately perform the duties involved in carrying on our mission as the servant church. A reasonable formula to use as a guideline would be a pastor for each group of 500 members. There is a need for an extension of our pastoral service, particularly if we are successful in trebling our membership in the next twenty-five years.

There should be a pastor who would devote his full time to a counseling service, to be on duty during the day and evening to meet with individuals who have personal problems. He should be trained in psychiatry and in all phases of counseling and have had special experience. Part of his time should be devoted to visiting the city workhouse, the juvenile court, and the city jail to counsel with unfortunate youngsters and adults who need help in time of trouble.

There should be three visitation pastors. One should devote his time calling on shut-ins and the sick in hospitals. Another should be a social service and welfare pastor who would devote his time to working with poverty and ethnic groups, since these are the people who need direction and guidance in solving their problems. The third should contact prospects for Membership in Central.

There should be a "Preacher of the Church" who would devote his entire time in the preparation of his sermons and other speeches to be delivered before organizations in the church or in the city. He should have time to study and travel. He should have years of parish ministry service to enable him to understand people, and never lose "the common touch."

It is suggested that the senior pastor devote his entire time as the administrative director of the congregation's program: to assign the duties of the pastoral staff and to supervise their activities; to work in close cooperation with the Minister of Music and the Business Executive; to act as consultant in prescribing the program and activities of the ten boards of the Ministry Program; to serve as ex officio member of all committees and boards to coordinate the overall program of the congregation; and to aid in formulating general policies involved in the operation of procedures and administration.

The youth program of the church has great potentials for Central and requires special staffing with a full-time director and assistants. Camp Amnicon has passed the early stages of development. No one can foretell all the possibilities for a building program, for acquiring additional land areas, and for operating almost a year-round program. Providing camping facilities for children of the inner city should continue to be a vital objective of Camp Amnicon. Here, too, there should be full-time directors with staff assistants.

No limitations should be placed on an adquate staff for the Parish Education Department. Of course, at present we have a Director of Parish Education who is responsible for the Sunday Church School, Confirmation, Vacation Church School, Adult Education, and the Bethel Bible Study Series. But with the anticipated growth in membership, all these phases of parish education will expand the enrollments. A division of responsibility must necessarily follow and I foresee an assistant full-time director, plus the organization of a volunteer staff to assist in this important religious training program of the church.

And, we cannot overlook the Central City concept as outlined in the American City Bureau survey with all its impact on the future of Central Lutheran Church. The proposal of "The Centrum" emphasizes the need to develop a comprehensive program of adult education for post-high school students and adults — a continuing program of education under Christian auspices. To provide the facilities for this program will mean that a fund-raising campaign for a considerable amount of money will be necessary.

In order to develop the total Central City concept, it is imperative that we continue in our program of land acquisition. It will be necessary to own the six-block area around the present structures in order to enable us to plan wisely for the development of Central City with parking facilities and a possible parking ramp. This is a priority need. We are hampered in our total realization of this project until all the required land has been acquired.

If the members are aware of their stewardship responsibilities, then they will be willing to provide for all the needs of Central on a pay-as-you-go basis, thus eliminating the need for mortgaging our future in these crucial times of economic and financial upheaval throughout the world.

I assume that you, as a reader, have asked the pertinent question, Where is the money coming from to pay for this enlarged and expansive program? The answer is simple and uncomplicated. Increase our membership as I have proposed, and the increased contributions will provide the necessary funds. If you study the table of budget and income figures, you can readily reach a conclusion that the Lord will provide. If the overall program of Central is challenging and effective in results, the contributions will come in. If our program is slipshod, careless and indifferent, the church will die on the vine and we will cease to exist.

But God has willed otherwise for Central Lutheran and we must accept his challenge. The record of the past proves that we have been blessed. The record of the future depends upon our courage and dedication now.

The needs of the church are challenging today. In troublous times like these, Christian people must support their churches and institutions.

In the seventeenth century, when war had bitterly divided the people of Britian, there was built the chapel of Staunton Harold in Leicestershire. The dedication inscription is there today, as a message for our own times:

"In the Year 1653

When all Things Sacred were Throughout Ye Nation

Either Demollisht or Profaned

Sir Robert Shirley, Barronet,

Founded this Church

Whose Singular Praise it is to Have Done

the Best Things

In Ye Worst Times

and

Hoped Them in the Most Calamitous"

APPENDIX

Presidents of the Congregation and Women's Guild
1919-1979

Year	Congregation	Woman's Guild
1919	J. A. O. Stub	Mrs. C. Wangaard
1920	J. A. O. Stub	Mrs. F. E. Moody
1921	J. A. O. Stub	Mrs. F. E. Moody
1922	C. O. Johnson	Mrs. F. E. Moody
1923	E. A. Rustad	Mrs. F. E. Moody
1924	Lars O. Rue	Mrs. F. E. Moody
1925	A. C. Tingdale	Mrs. Oliver Prestholdt
1926	Lars O. Rue	Mrs. J. T. Neadle
1927	Lars O. Rue	Mrs. F. E. Moody
1928	E. A. Rustad	Mrs. F. E. Moody
1929	E. A. Rustad	Mrs. L. O. Rue
1930	S. J. Syverson	Mrs. W. H. Jensen
1931	O. T. Rishoff	Mrs. Charles Howe
1932	O. A. Hohle	Mrs. Julie Kintzinger
1933	T. S. Lyndal	Mrs. L. P. Westrum
1934	G. E. Strate	Mrs. L. P. Westrum
1935	G. L. Holm	Mrs. L. P. Westrum
1936	C. C. Thronson	Mrs. L. P. Westrum
1937	C. A. Stiehm	Mrs. L. P. Westrum
1938	Barney Anderson	Mrs. Chas. A. Thiele
1939	Dr. J. C. Giere	Mrs. Emil Johansen
1940	T. O. Berge	Mrs. Emil Johansen
1941	C. E. Larson	Mrs. A. F. Beier
1942	E. W. Schlappritzi	Mrs. Clay W. Johnson
1943	Arthur R. Hustad	Mrs. Clay W. Johnson

1944	Arthur R. Hustad	Mrs. Clay W. Johnson
1945	Arthur R. Hustad	Mrs. Oliver Prestholdt
1946	A. C. Wangaard	Mrs. Oliver Prestholdt
1947	A. C. Wangaard	Mrs. L. W. Ahlness
1948	Burch N. Bell	Mrs. J. E. Hogander
1949	Jos. T. Sydness	Mrs. J. E. Hogander
1950	Jos. T. Sydness	Mrs. Reuben H. Lee
1951	P. Don Carson	Mrs. Reuben H. Lee
1952	P. Don Carson	Mrs. C. S. Nelson
1953	Harold C. Anderson	Mrs. C. S. Nelson
1954	Harold C. Hoel	Mrs. H. A. Bitzer
1955	Harold C. Hoel	Mrs. H. A. Bitzer
1956	Cato C. Ennis	Mrs. Olendo M. Olson
1957	Cato C. Ennis	Mrs. Olendo M. Olson
1958	John R. Winsor	Mrs. Guy O. Tollerud
1959	Franic W. Gaasedelen	Mrs. Guy O. Tollerud
1960	Guy O. Tollerud	Mrs. E. E. Ohsberg
1961	Leon Haaland	Mrs. E. E. Ohsberg
1962	Elmer N. Olson	Mrs. Hilda Emmons
1963	Glen B. Gore	Mrs. Hilda Emmons
1964	Milo S. Mickelson	Miss Edna Sorenson
1965	Robert M. L. Lindquist	Mrs. Arthur Holt
1966	Glen V. Hoople	Mrs. Norman Hemry
1967	Donald A. Olson	Mrs. Norman Hemry
1968	Dr. Robert Cooper	Mrs. C. Donald Carlson
1969	Orville Thompson	Mrs. Michael Elnicky
1970	Mr. Glenn H. Steinke	Mrs. Martha Bondhus
1971	Mr. Merlin Hovden	Mrs. Merlin B. Hovden
1972	Mr. James A. Halls	Miss Mildred Martinson
1973	Mr. Wm. A. Benson, Jr.	Mrs. George Armitage

1974	Dr. Thomas Hoffmann	Mrs. George Armitage
1975	Mr. Robert J. Jung	Mrs. Lloyd Dale
1976	Mr. Richard Brestrup	Mrs. Lloyd Dale
1977	Mr. Richard H. Hilden	Mrs. John Bachman
1978	Mr. Richard H. Hilden	Mrs. John Bachman
1979	Mr. Robert E. Christenson	Mrs. Ernest Pudas